ALSO BY ROBERT LOWELL

Land of Unlikeness (1944)

Lord Weary's Castle (1946)

The Mills of the Kavanaughs (1951)

Life Studies (1959)

Phaedra (translation) (1961)

Imitations (1961)

For the Union Dead (1964)

The Old Glory (plays) (1965)

Near the Ocean (1967)

The Voyage & Other Versions of Poems by Baudelaire (1969)

Prometheus Bound (translation) (1969)

Notebook 1967–68 (1969) (*Notebook*, revised and expanded edition, 1970)

History (1973)

For Lizzie and Harriet (1973)

The Dolphin (1973)

Selected Poems (1976) (revised edition, 1977)

Day by Day (1977)

The Oresteia of Aeschylus (translation) (1978)

Collected Prose (1987)

Collected Poems (2003)

The Letters of Robert Lowell (2007)

Selected Poems (2007)

New Selected Poems

ROBERT LOWELL

New Selected Poems

EDITED BY KATIE PETERSON

FARRAR, STRAUS AND GIROUX   NEW YORK

Farrar, Straus and Giroux
18 West 18th Street, New York 10011

Printed in the United States of America
First edition, 2017

Library of Congress Control Number: 2016956347
ISBN: 978-0-374-25133-8

Designed by Jonathan D. Lippincott

www.fsgbooks.com
www.twitter.com/fsgbooks • www.facebook.com/fsgbooks

10 9 8 7 6 5 4 3 2

Contents

Introduction

In his time, Robert Lowell achieved unquestionable stardom. The author of twelve collections, countless translations, adaptations from Greek plays, and an original drama, he won the Pulitzer in 1947 for his second book, *Lord Weary's Castle*, and again in 1974 for his penultimate collection, *The Dolphin* (one of three books he published in 1973 alone). Neither of these collections, though, brought him the fame of his fourth volume, *Life Studies* (1959), which includes an exquisitely matter-of-fact prose memoir of growing up in Boston as the son of a Brahmin family in decline and a series of family portraits written in a detail-rich, sensually baroque free verse many poets have imitated but none have matched. *Life Studies*, with its candor and intimacy, may have invented "personal" poetry—it may also be the one collection of Lowell's that twenty-first-century readers have heard of—but he refused to brand his patent with repetition. His subsequent books each attempt something new. The formal virtuosity paired with his social pedigree to form a legend of achievement. The poetry critic Edmund Wilson, whose own former stature as a literary journalist seems nearly unimaginable in contemporary culture, deemed Lowell one of only two poets in the twentieth century able to achieve a career "on the old nineteenth-century scale." In 2017, forty years after his death, one fears Lowell remains known for precisely that.

I write this at a time when many individuals with many different kinds of lives aspire to be poets, and many different kinds of poetry are said to thrive in these United States. Is it too easy to say that Lowell's star has fallen a bit? Or is it actually that the sense of achievement his work self-consciously carries with it itself carries less credibility than it used to? I arrived in Cambridge, Massachusetts, in the fall of 1997 to earn a doctorate in English at

Harvard, a university that claims Lowell both as undergraduate dropout and as professor. Raised in the San Francisco Bay Area, I cut my teeth on the Beat Generation and drum circles and didn't know anyone who lived where they were "from." In my adopted Massachusetts, Lowell's work was everywhere—and it was a complete mystery to me. The poet Elizabeth Bishop, teaching in Seattle, writes to her close friend Lowell, ". . . my 'class' is finding you very difficult & much too EASTERN!— &, save me, they won't look up words, even the easiest, in the dictionary . . ." I was one of them. Though I didn't mind looking up things in the dictionary, those definitions don't help you see what something's for. A Lowell poem presented a thicket of allusions: "There were no tickets for that altitude / once held by Hellas, when the Goddess stood, / prince, pope, philosopher and golden bough, / pure mind and murder at the scything prow— / Minerva, the miscarriage of the brain" ("Beyond the Alps"). I wanted to read poetry of the present and the future, not the past. If there were no tickets for that altitude, why did I have to watch him on the downslope?

Years later, far from Boston, I heard Lowell's former student Alan Williamson read a poem with an unassuming title, "The Day." From the last volume Lowell collected and published in his lifetime, *Day by Day*, it begins this way:

> It's amazing
> the day is still here
> like lightning on an open field,
> terra firma and transient
> swimming in variation,
> fresh as when man first broke
> like the crocus all over the earth.

The voice of the poem came straight from a human body, in the middle of an ordinary day. Indeed, the voice seemed to have only the existence of the day as its problem, as in that ordinary question asked between friends, or lovers, or even strangers uncomfortable with their strangeness, "How was your day?" That voice understood the randomness of fortune and the strangeness of human persistence as if it were as given as the sky. Relaxed in the midst of chaos, the voice of "The Day" knew, in equal measures, ritual and surprise. The energy of its similes had something to do with a terrified joy—the only kind I believe in without question. You don't need to know what Modernism did to poetry to feel how the project of twenty-first-century life means following through on the great social changes of the twentieth century—you just need to check Facebook and see how many times we need to be liked to get up in the morning. In this poem, and in others in *Day by Day*, all of Modernism—which mourns, celebrates, and obsesses over our alienation from a collective narrative readers past, present, and future all once shared—became the problem of just having a day, our day, a human day, so beautifully and terrifyingly to ourselves. This Lowell defies achievement. This Lowell knows better than to think what's lasting is any more than a dare. This Lowell understands that former ways of life cannot simply be returned to, ever. This Lowell is not in denial about a past that has passed away. The day, in this poem and in others, manifests the vulnerable predicament of what we once called the Enlightenment and what we might now identify as the beginning of getting "woke." And now that a climate change that not everyone believes in has wrecked the seasons, the day might be all we have left together as ritual.

The Robert Lowell I offer in this brief selection emphasizes the perishability of life, its twinned quality of fragility and repetition, as framed by the structured evanescence of daily consciousness. The problem of the human person here is the difficulty and promise of having a good day. Like a good poem, a good day is harder to achieve than we realize but revelatory when it's given. Of course, I was wrong about Lowell that first time. It turns out he'd been writing these poems all along—the first poem included in this book is "New Year's Day," and the last, "Summer Tides," takes place at the end of a day seen as a metaphor for a life. So often, in these poems, the day and the fact of its running out form all the drama the poem needs:

> . . . The clocks
> Are tolling. I am dying. The shocked stones
> Are falling like a ton of bricks and bones
> That snap and splinter and descend in glass
> Before a priest who mumbles through his Mass
> And sprinkles holy water; and the Day
> Breaks with its lighting on the man of clay . . .
> ("Between the Porch and the Altar")

> In between the limits of day,
> hours and hours go by under the crew haircuts
> and slightly too little nonsensical bachelor twinkle
> of the Roman Catholic attendants.
> ("Waking in the Blue")

> I lay all day on my bed.
> I chain-smoked through the night,
> learning to flinch
> at the flash of the matchlight.
> ("Eye and Tooth")

> Downstairs, you correct notes at the upright piano,
> twice upright this midday Sunday torn from the whole
> green cloth of summer . . .
> ("Summer")

> Bright sun of my bright day,
> I thank God for being alive—
> a way of writing I once thought heartless.
> ("Logan Airport, Boston")

My favorite Lowell poems are not flickers of consciousness, em-
blems of the merely spontaneous, but whole days lived through,
entire days survived—they have a sense of beginning and ending,
the trauma of morning and the held-out possibility of recovery.
Contemporary American poets revere—and teach, far more of-
ten than Lowell—the more consciously "hip" work of his near-
contemporary Frank O'Hara and the poets of the New York
School, whose plentiful charms turn moments into fantasies of on-
going luminosity. Lowell, on the other hand, offers us days rather
than moments, hangovers (and their flashbacks) rather than lunch
hours, divorces (and their entanglements) rather than engage-
ments, the morning after rather than the party. He offers no fan-
tasy of a clean slate: "Death's not an event in life, it's not lived
through" ("Plotted"). He doesn't simply live—he lives through.

I began with the landmark *Collected Poems*, edited by Frank
Bidart and David Gewanter, and *Notebook 1967–68*, a volume
Lowell expanded and retitled simply *Notebook* in 1970, and soon
after transformed into the two collections *History* and *For Lizzie
and Harriet*. The original *Notebook 1967–68* stands alone in its vi-
vacity and initial impulse, and the two collections it becomes exist
alongside rather than instead of it. Lowell's significant reworking
of the original *Notebook* into a revised edition and then two sep-
arate published collections should be viewed less as an editorial
problem than as a significant manifestation of a lifelong practice.
Lowell "began again" many times—he accuses himself in the
voice of the poet Randall Jarrell, "you didn't write, you *re*wrote.'"
It is quite literally true. He buried his first book, *Land of Unlike-
ness*, resurrecting the best poems for his second. In the index to
the *Collected Poems*, titles reappear, telling in their simplicity, both
as preoccupations and as perennial hopes for a fresh start: "Mar-
riage," "Hospital," Lowell's infamous nickname, "Caligula," and
various permutations of "Summer," several of which I've included
here. I've also included two poems, "Pastime" from the revised
edition of *Notebook* (1970) and "Bobby Delano" from *History*, that
might be seen as versions of the same poem, different approaches

to the same material. Lowell devoted the middle of his career to the sonnet, reshaping several poems and translations in the process. The sonnet's brevity and closure offered freedom as much as confinement—especially if, like Lowell, you could just do it again. And why not? It was as if a new poem was a new day—or was it that any new day compelled the poet to begin again? The magnificent last poems of *Day by Day* are not Lowell's liberation into free verse—they're his continuation of the sonnet by other means. They feel like stretched-out, luxurious sonnets, and their uncertain endings often come after an equally uncertain turn, the equivalent of a closing volta.

I wanted to hear Lowell's career as a voice, to capture this sense of living in time in a human-scale, lively way. To try to do this for Robert Lowell is to wreck the monument and begin again. To read the poems, and truly hear the voice, is to discover that he'd been wrecking the monument all along. As the great poet of the human day, he understood perishability more than I'd at first given him credit for.

The challenge in editing a brief selection in this case can be easily stated as a numbers game: the *Collected* stands at 988 and *Notebook 1967–68* at 156, and this collection is 234 pages. But these numbers can't tell the story. A selection also turns Lowell's life back into a series of days. I made no attempt to be comprehensive and instead selected poems for their energy and persistence. I chose the poet's best days and found that repeated tasks of description give them literal shape—portrait, self-portrait, landscape. Those tasks became couched in devotion to the day itself, and to the energy of being present in it. The poems begin in prayer (in *Lord Weary's Castle*, where Catholic emblems seem, finally, to be nothing more than sensual delights) and end there (in *Day by Day*, where Lowell fiercely tries to actually pray). The last poems pray authentically, that is to say, to an unverifiable god. In this way, they push the limits of realism (as style and stance), using the wilder energy of desire.

With Lowell, the challenge of selecting not simply the best

poems but poems that make sense together presents itself vividly, because the work adheres so closely to the life. He was the first poet to be called "confessional," and though he didn't like the term, it gets right the poetry's sense of breaking through a public surface into a hoard of personal material. Disclosure, in Lowell, manifests as equal parts ritual and chaos. In the work, those Lowell knew and lived with exert the rights of persons; I grew concerned that I'd favored his daughter, Harriet, over his son, Sheridan. I worried that his third wife, Caroline, didn't get enough space. I reconsidered the question of his own day, whether he had done wrong to excerpt his second wife's letters in *The Dolphin*, a book that tells of their breakup—a decision that lost him the friendship of the great feminist poet Adrienne Rich. I wanted the reader to see the importance of his friendship with another poet, Elizabeth Bishop, an intimacy that stewarded many of Lowell's poems, including two of his greatest, "Skunk Hour" and "Thanks-Offering for Recovery." I worried that the events of the life would lose focus, that the reader wouldn't know everything that happened about the poet who wrote: "why not say what happened?" ("Epilogue").

But I also wanted to choose poems memorable for their language, not simply the vanishing facts of story. I wanted to show how Lowell remained constitutionally immune to any stultifying permanence either of form or of spirit—an immunity that emboldens his diction, both because he lived a life so close to the poems and because he heard and felt a world much larger than his one particular life. The best poems stay a little messy. The language of their day, likewise, is not simply the language of the day—Lowell had little or no truck with our contemporary penchant for the idea that the way we write must be the way we talk. The language of the day of the poem meant, for Lowell, any language that worked: any language the day required. His best poems show an untidy love for all kinds of language as they strain to find unity. In "Mermaid," Lowell quotes Baudelaire and ventriloquizes Muhammad Ali. Poems even a reader of Lowell might not be familiar with, such as the gorgeous "Suburban Surf," show the effortlessness that results when this unity is actually found. That famous line from "Epilogue" mentioned above stands, in the poem, after a moment of self-doubt that's also an adequate characterization of what the vast ranges of speech make accessible in our diverse world:

> But sometimes everything I write
> with the threadbare art of my eye
> seems a snapshot,
> lurid, rapid, garish, grouped,
> heightened from life,
> yet paralyzed by fact.
> All's misalliance.

Diverse languages, misallied, do more than reflect the confusions of our lives captured within technology—they show us how human experience, diverse and divergent, would never be the same again. Lowell's work shows us how the information explosion of the Internet fulfills a prophecy of chaos rather than creates it.

Being willing to be uncomfortable is a power in poetry— something to be praised, something that helps us see. The misalliances Lowell heard and felt as part of being so deeply in the present tense make his poems complicated sometimes, jumpy sometimes, nervous. But those misalliances also helped him make language. In "The Day," he coins a word to describe being in time:

> when we lived momently
> together forever
> in love with our nature—

"The day" is where we can live "momently" together, in whatever way presents itself, and the best of Lowell's poems place us energetically and uncomfortably there.

Recently, a friend suggested that American strangers ask the question "How's your day going?" as a way of not asking the question "Where are you from?" "Where are you from" seems, on the surface, friendly enough, but its answers have always been divisive: "Are you from the same place I'm from?" "Were you born here?" Maybe it doesn't matter where you're from; maybe it matters more how your day's going—that is, where you actually are. Lowell's translation of the Brunetto Latini canto of Dante's *Inferno*, which I have excerpted in this collection, makes immediate the predicament of Dante's beloved teacher, consigned to hell with other condemned scholars, who are also sodomites, guilty of lust. Latini's real crime seems to be understanding too well the world's rapacious appetite for judging others. Ezra Pound, Modernism's genius advocate for vernacular speech in poetry who spent years confined to a mental institution after espousing Fascist politics during the Second World War, praised Lowell's rendering. In a ghostly recording, an aging Pound, back in the world at last but discredited in the public eye, recites a portion of the translation in a hoarse, low whisper. In Lowell's version, Latini speaks to Dante in a brutally accented English that feels like a critique of political speech, and those who are tricked by it, after our recent election year: "Let the pack / run loose, and sicken on the carcasses / that heap the streets, but spare the tender flower, / if one should rise above the swamp and mess." To "update" a classic means to let it keep finding us where we are.

It remains, nevertheless, true that Lowell's work once made the question "Where are you from" the order of the day. This question governed his early style, so laced with New England atmosphere it approaches kitsch. A detail-oriented apparent accuracy suffuses the portraits and self-portraits of *Life Studies*, a book full of days-in-the-life of Lowell and his family. Teeming with places, dates, and their material corollaries, things, and their more literary cousins, allusions, the poems of *Life Studies* also overflow with proper names (in both senses): 91 Revere Street, Beverly Farms, Boston's "hardly passionate Marlborough Street," L.L.Bean, Blue

Hill, Rapallo, Jonathan Edwards, Murder Incorporated, and Czar Lepke:

> I was so out of things, I'd never heard
> of the Jehovah's Witnesses.
> "Are you a C.O.?" I asked a fellow jailbird.
> "No," he answered, "I'm a J.W."
>   ("Memories of West Street and Lepke")

But here, facts are married to confusion—a Jehovah's Witness starts as an unrecognizable J.W. and ends as a "jailbird." Writes Lowell in *Notebook*, "dates fade faster than we do." By the way, a C.O. is a conscientious objector, and Lowell's conversion to Catholicism made him one in the Second World War, for more than a few days in his life, for a year—but for the purpose of his art, only for a poem or two. Whoever Robert Lowell really was, his poems remember how many times he changed who he was.

In Lowell's poetry, no two days are alike—time moves on. We don't always remember the fact, but we are nearly always seared by the way a fact feels. Randall Jarrell said that Elizabeth Bishop's work was marked by the conviction "I have seen it"; Lowell's radiates with the vaguer credibility "I have felt it," emotional and somatic. Felt in the body, one's understood context becomes unstable: "I keep no rank nor station. / Cured, I am frizzled, stale and small" ("Home After Three Months Away"). Lowell could find real knowledge only in the earthly, the biographical. In poetry, now, we take this for granted—how many volumes are prized for their "personal story," individually held but collectively validated, structured not simply by suffering but by some assumed faith in the reader's response to it? But Lowell took a different view of the relationship between personal experience and knowledge. Just because the facts of the life provided the only basis for what could be known in poetry didn't mean you could know very much.

> I meant to write about our last walk.
> We had nothing to do but gaze—

seven years, now nothing but a diverting smile,
dalliance by a river, a speeding swan . . .
the misleading promise
to last with joy as long as our bodies,
nostalgia pulverized by thought,
nomadic as yesterday's whirling snow,
all whiteness splotched.

("Last Walk?")

In this sense, Lowell is still ahead of his time, or at least outside it.
To assert both that personal experience was the only way you could
know anything and that you couldn't really know very much that
way is to see the "freedom" of contemporary experience as both vi-
brantly lived and meaningfully limited. Such a perspective leaves one
very much stranded in the present, by which I mean, facing reality.

•

In a certain political neighborhood of our contemporary world,
we like to use the word "privilege" to describe people such as
Lowell—white, male, funded, educated, carriers of social position
and family name (two of his cousins were notable American poets,
and his mother descended from a Constitution signer). Lately, in
American poetry, we like not liking people like that, and we dis-
trust privilege as we would a mask. But on the human level, birth
is an accident:

In the grandiloquent lettering on Mother's coffin,
Lowell had been misspelled *LOVEL*.
The corpse
was wrapped like *panettone* in Italian tinfoil.

("Sailing Home from Rapallo")

Death fades family names and disintegrates the hallmarks of pres-
tige, and privilege can't help you see. Lowell's best work knows

this. The poetic tradition has its own relationship with privilege: the history of poetry, crudely seen for years, was the history of those with the power and leisure to write it, white men. Lowell easily found his place in this history of poetry while he was alive. Maybe it's time to let his work teach us about the history of the person instead. Lowell's sonnet about Robert Frost from *History* has something to do with both—the poem crosses a moment of poetic inheritance with personal feeling. Lowell's trying to find words for the actual mania he suffered, and it throws the expected patriarchal bonding with Frost a bit off-kilter:

> Robert Frost at midnight, the audience gone
> to vapor, the great act laid on the shelf in mothballs,
> his voice is musical and raw—he writes in the flyleaf:
> *For Robert from Robert, his friend in the art.*
> "Sometimes I feel too full of myself," I say.
> And he, misunderstanding, "When I am low,
> I stray away . . ."

The poem ends with Lowell still trying to be understood—

> And I, "Sometimes I'm so happy I can't stand myself."
> And he, "When I am too full of joy, I think
> how little good my health did anyone near me."
>
> ("Robert Frost")

Frost does, in a sense, understand Lowell at the end. Though the sonnet is a moving testimony about the stigma of speaking about mental illness, it's also something else—a displaced self-portrait in dialogue, a reckoning with how poetic privilege, prestige, renown, and the rest don't translate into the kind of capital that builds life. Even "health," the one privilege Lowell lacked (bipolar, he was hospitalized fourteen times for mania and once for depression), doesn't add up to the kind of knowledge you can use that other people can necessarily share. He writes later toward his family, essentially rephrasing these lines of Frost's: ". . . When most happiest / how do I know I can keep any of us alive?" ("Wild-rose" from "Another Summer").

Nothing of "privilege" can mask Lowell's authentic sense of his own limitations in his best poems. He relies not on "privilege" but on awareness to steady him through changes. He experiences knowledge, like the passage of time, as something withstood rather than possessed. Lowell's signature sonic move was to turn the line in skilled but sudden enjambment, a break in the middle of a sense-unit. A reader hears it everywhere: "the audience gone / to vapor." Such discord refuses the feeling of certainty in any poem; it can even approach one of the signature emotions of our times, fear. The family portraits of *Life Studies* come to a close with an eerie nocturne from blue-blooded Castine, Maine, "Skunk Hour," dedicated to a friend, not a relative—Bishop. If you knew Lowell before picking up this *New Selected Poems*, you probably knew him from these lines:

> I myself am hell;
> nobody's here—

But you can see him better in the ones that follow:

> only skunks, that search
> in the moonlight for a bite to eat.
> They march on their soles up Main Street:
> white stripes, moonstruck eyes' red fire
> under the chalk-dry and spar spire
> of the Trinitarian Church.
>
> I stand on top
> of our back steps and breathe the rich air—
> a mother skunk with her column of kittens swills the
>   garbage pail.
> She jabs her wedge-head in a cup

of sour cream, drops her ostrich tail,
and will not scare.

You can see him better as he sees himself—as a skunk. What he can't see—the skunk's head covered in whiteness—is what he is. It's easy enough to read the skunk symbolically and credit Lowell with a poetic understanding of the foul way privilege can mask an understanding of the world in which white has masked black faces and bodies in destructive ways. To me, this is child's play compared with how Lowell gets us to a possible place for self-recognition. He's staring at an ordinary pest in his garbage, at the end of the day, in the midst of habit. The end of the poem corrects an ordinary narcissism—he thought he was the only one there, and discovers he's not. He remembers the skunk as a "somebody"; the animal world marks his return to the ethical. He's not just trying to see what he can't see but admitting that he can't see, after an entire poem about looking at a familiar view from an owned vantage point. At the end of the day, what is he doing on top of his back steps, if not "checking his privilege," or at least imagining what it might look like if he could? In Lowell's centennial year, the year of the inauguration of Donald Trump, I value this poem because it shows a white man willing to stay uncomfortable in the midst of change and uncertainty—a human person choosing the vulnerability of sharing a world rather than the deceiving strength of owning or partitioning one. The poet Christina Davis has pointed out to me that "Skunk Hour," the title of the poem, is easily reversed to "our skunk," a poetic form of ownership that actually makes possible a kind of "owning up."

The events of Lowell's actual biography made him give up a sense that his life would be either healthy or straightforward. His imagination enabled him to create work that still matters to us, none of whose lives seem, at this point, to be easily recognizable as either. His poems about mental illness anticipate a twenty-first-century culture in which having a diagnosis has become as overstated and necessary as having a college degree. In the best of these, illness refuses to pigeonhole itself as disability or dramatize itself as a privilege of the artist. "Notice," from *Day by Day*, passes into the twenty-first century familiar to anyone who's ever mistaken a medical professional for someone who can tell you the meaning of life:

> The resident doctor said,
> "We are not deep in ideas, imagination or enthusiasm—
> how can we help you?"
> I asked,
> "These days of only poems and depression—
> what can I do with them?
> Will they help me to notice
> what I cannot bear to look at?"
>
> ("Notice")

A poem like this doesn't only anticipate a world in which no "normal" exists, either in psychological condition or in life plan: it imagines a world in which the idea of "the normal" has been almost forgotten. Nowhere is this understanding more moving than in Lowell's treatment of his complicated family life, in *Notebook*, *For Lizzie and Harriet*, and especially *The Dolphin*, with his last two marriages braided together in time with children and stepchildren and across an ocean. Don't we all wish we—or someone—could have planned our lives better? Lowell admits that feeling and lets it go. He stands vividly in the midst of experience, when all we'd thought we'd known demands to be known again. The final lines of "Notice" remind us how bravely Lowell stood in his own discomfort: "Then home—I can walk it blindfold. / But we most notice— / we are designed for the moment."

Katie Peterson
Albany, California

from

Lord Weary's Castle

(1942)

New Year's Day

Again and then again . . . the year is born
To ice and death, and it will never do
To skulk behind storm-windows by the stove
To hear the postgirl sounding her French horn
When the thin tidal ice is wearing through.
Here is the understanding not to love
Our neighbor, or tomorrow that will sieve
Our resolutions. While we live, we live

To snuff the smoke of victims. In the snow
The kitten heaved its hindlegs, as if fouled,
And died. We bent it in a Christmas box
And scattered blazing weeds to scare the crow
Until the snake-tailed sea-winds coughed and howled
For alms outside the church whose double locks
Wait for St. Peter, the distorted key.
Under St. Peter's bell the parish sea

Swells with its smelt into the burlap shack
Where Joseph plucks his hand-lines like a harp,
And hears the fearful *Puer natus est*
Of Circumcision, and relives the wrack
And howls of Jesus whom he holds. How sharp
The burden of the Law before the beast:
Time and the grindstone and the knife of God.
The Child is born in blood, O child of blood.

The Quaker Graveyard in Nantucket

(FOR WARREN WINSLOW, DEAD AT SEA)

Let man have dominion over the fishes of the sea and the fowls of the air and the beasts and the whole earth, and every creeping creature that moveth upon the earth.

I.

A brackish reach of shoal off Madaket,—
The sea was still breaking violently and night
Had steamed into our North Atlantic Fleet,
When the drowned sailor clutched the drag-net. Light
Flashed from his matted head and marble feet,
He grappled at the net
With the coiled, hurdling muscles of his thighs:
The corpse was bloodless, a botch of reds and whites,
Its open, staring eyes
Were lustreless dead-lights
Or cabin-windows on a stranded hulk
Heavy with sand. We weight the body, close
Its eyes and heave it seaward whence it came,
Where the heel-headed dogfish barks its nose
On Ahab's void and forehead; and the name
Is blocked in yellow chalk.
Sailors, who pitch this portent at the sea
Where dreadnaughts shall confess
Its hell-bent deity,
When you are powerless
To sand-bag this Atlantic bulwark, faced
By the earth-shaker, green, unwearied, chaste
In his steel scales: ask for no Orphean lute
To pluck life back. The guns of the steeled fleet
Recoil and then repeat
The hoarse salute.

II.

Whenever winds are moving and their breath
Heaves at the roped-in bulwarks of this pier,
The terns and sea-gulls tremble at your death
In these home waters. Sailor, can you hear
The Pequod's sea wings, beating landward, fall
Headlong and break on our Atlantic wall
Off 'Sconset, where the yawing S-boats splash
The bellbuoy, with ballooning spinnakers,
As the entangled, screeching mainsheet clears
The blocks: off Madaket, where lubbers lash
The heavy surf and throw their long lead squids
For blue-fish? Sea-gulls blink their heavy lids
Seaward. The winds' wings beat upon the stones,
Cousin, and scream for you and the claws rush
At the sea's throat and wring it in the slush
Of this old Quaker graveyard where the bones
Cry out in the long night for the hurt beast
Bobbing by Ahab's whaleboats in the East.

III.

All you recovered from Poseidon died
With you, my cousin, and the harrowed brine
Is fruitless on the blue beard of the god,
Stretching beyond us to the castles in Spain,
Nantucket's westward haven. To Cape Cod
Guns, cradled on the tide,
Blast the eelgrass about a waterclock
Of bilge and backwash, roil the salt and sand
Lashing earth's scaffold, rock
Our warships in the hand
Of the great God, where time's contrition blues
Whatever it was these Quaker sailors lost
In the mad scramble of their lives. They died

When time was open-eyed,
Wooden and childish; only bones abide
There, in the nowhere, where their boats were tossed
Sky-high, where mariners had fabled news
Of IS, the whited monster. What it cost
Them is their secret. In the sperm-whale's slick
I see the Quakers drown and hear their cry:
"If God himself had not been on our side,
If God himself had not been on our side,
When the Atlantic rose against us, why,
Then it had swallowed us up quick."

IV.
This is the end of the whaleroad and the whale
Who spewed Nantucket bones on the thrashed swell
And stirred the troubled waters to whirlpools
To send the Pequod packing off to hell:
This is the end of them, three-quarters fools,
Snatching at straws to sail
Seaward and seaward on the turntail whale,
Spouting out blood and water as it rolls,
Sick as a dog to these Atlantic shoals:
Clamavimus, O depths. Let the sea-gulls wail

For water, for the deep where the high tide
Mutters to its hurt self, mutters and ebbs.
Waves wallow in their wash, go out and out,
Leave only the death-rattle of the crabs,
The beach increasing, its enormous snout
Sucking the ocean's side.
This is the end of running on the waves;
We are poured out like water. Who will dance
The mast-lashed master of Leviathans
Up from this field of Quakers in their unstoned graves?

V.

When the whale's viscera go and the roll
Of its corruption overruns this world
Beyond tree-swept Nantucket and Woods Hole
And Martha's Vineyard, Sailor, will your sword
Whistle and fall and sink into the fat?
In the great ash-pit of Jehoshaphat
The bones cry for the blood of the white whale,
The fat flukes arch and whack about its ears,
The death-lance churns into the sanctuary, tears
The gun-blue swingle, heaving like a flail,
And hacks the coiling life out: it works and drags
And rips the sperm-whale's midriff into rags,
Gobbets of blubber spill to wind and weather,
Sailor, and gulls go round the stoven timbers
Where the morning stars sing out together
And thunder shakes the white surf and dismembers
The red flag hammered in the mast-head. Hide
Our steel, Jonas Messias, in Thy side.

VI.

OUR LADY OF WALSINGHAM

There once the penitents took off their shoes
And then walked barefoot the remaining mile;
And the small trees, a stream and hedgerows file
Slowly along the munching English lane,
Like cows to the old shrine, until you lose
Track of your dragging pain.
The stream flows down under the druid tree,
Shiloah's whirlpools gurgle and make glad
The castle of God. Sailor, you were glad
And whistled Sion by that stream. But see:

Our Lady, too small for her canopy,
Sits near the altar. There's no comeliness
At all or charm in that expressionless
Face with its heavy eyelids. As before,
This face, for centuries a memory,
Non est species, neque decor,
Expressionless, expresses God: it goes
Past castled Sion. She knows what God knows,
Not Calvary's Cross nor crib at Bethlehem
Now, and the world shall come to Walsingham.

VII.

The empty winds are creaking and the oak
Splatters and splatters on the cenotaph,
The boughs are trembling and a gaff
Bobs on the untimely stroke
Of the greased wash exploding on a shoal-bell
In the old mouth of the Atlantic. It's well;
Atlantic, you are fouled with the blue sailors,
Sea-monsters, upward angel, downward fish:
Unmarried and corroding, spare of flesh
Mart once of supercilious, wing'd clippers,
Atlantic, where your bell-trap guts its spoil
You could cut the brackish winds with a knife
Here in Nantucket, and cast up the time
When the Lord God formed man from the sea's slime
And breathed into his face the breath of life,
And blue-lung'd combers lumbered to the kill.
The Lord survives the rainbow of His will.

Buttercups

When we were children our papas were stout
And colorless as seaweed or the floats
At anchor off New Bedford. We were shut
In gardens where our brassy sailor coats
Made us like black-eyed susans bending out
Into the ocean. Then my teeth were cut:
A levelled broom-pole butt
Was pushed into my thin
And up-turned chin—
There were shod hoofs behind the horseplay. But
I played Napoleon in my attic cell
Until my shouldered broom
Bobbed down the room
With horse and neighing shell.

Recall the shadows the doll-curtains veined
On Ancrem Winslow's ponderous plate from blue
China, the breaking of time's haggard tide
On the huge cobwebbed print of Waterloo,
With a cracked smile across the glass. I cried
To see the Emperor's sabered eagle slide
From the clutching grenadier
Staff-officer
With the gold leaf cascading down his side—
A red dragoon, his plough-horse rearing, swayed
Back on his reins to crop
The buttercup
Bursting upon the braid.

Between the Porch and the Altar

I.

MOTHER AND SON

Meeting his mother makes him lose ten years,
Or is it twenty? Time, no doubt, has ears
That listen to the swallowed serpent, wound
Into its bowels, but he thinks no sound
Is possible before her, he thinks the past
Is settled. It is honest to hold fast
Merely to what one sees with one's own eyes
When the red velvet curves and haunches rise
To blot him from the pretty driftwood fire's
Façade of welcome. Then the son retires
Into the sack and selfhood of the boy
Who clawed through fallen houses of his Troy,
Homely and human only when the flames
Crackle in recollection. Nothing shames
Him more than this uncoiling, counterfeit
Body presented as an idol. It
Is something in a circus, big as life,
The painted dragon, a mother and a wife
With flat glass eyes pushed at him on a stick;
The human mover crawls to make them click.
The forehead of her father's portrait peels
With rosy dryness, and the schoolboy kneels
To ask the benediction of the hand,
Lifted as though to motion him to stand,
Dangling its watch-chain on the Holy Book—
A little golden snake that mouths a hook.

II.

ADAM AND EVE

The Farmer sizzles on his shaft all day.
He is content and centuries away
From white-hot Concord, and he stands on guard.
Or is he melting down like sculptured lard?
His hand is crisp and steady on the plough.
I quarrelled with you, but am happy now
To while away my life for your unrest
Of terror. Never to have lived is best;
Man tasted Eve with death. I taste my wife
And children while I hold your hands. I knife
Their names into this elm. What is exempt?
I eye the statue with an awed contempt
And see the puritanical façade
Of the white church that Irish exiles made
For Patrick—that Colonial from Rome
Had magicked the charmed serpents from their home,
As though he were the Piper. Will his breath
Scorch the red dragon of my nerves to death?
By sundown we are on a shore. You walk
A little way before me and I talk,
Half to myself and half aloud. They lied,
My cold-eyed seedy fathers when they died,
Or rather threw their lives away, to fix
Sterile, forbidding nameplates on the bricks
Above a kettle. Jesus rest their souls!
You cry for help. Your market-basket rolls
With all its baking apples in the lake.
You watch the whorish slither of a snake
That chokes a duckling. When we try to kiss,
Our eyes are slits and cringing, and we hiss;
Scales glitter on our bodies as we fall.
The Farmer melts upon his pedestal.

III.

KATHERINE'S DREAM

It must have been a Friday. I could hear
The top-floor typist's thunder and the beer
That you had brought in cases hurt my head;
I'd sent the pillows flying from my bed,
I hugged my knees together and I gasped.
The dangling telephone receiver rasped
Like someone in a dream who cannot stop
For breath or logic till his victim drop
To darkness and the sheets. I must have slept,
But still could hear my father who had kept
Your guilty presents but cut off my hair.
He whispers that he really doesn't care
If I am your kept woman all my life,
Or ruin your two children and your wife;
But my dishonor makes him drink. Of course
I'll tell the court the truth for his divorce.
I walk through snow into St. Patrick's yard.
Black nuns with glasses smile and stand on guard
Before a bulkhead in a bank of snow,
Whose charred doors open, as good people go
Inside by twos to the confessor. One
Must have a friend to enter there, but none
Is friendless in this crowd, and the nuns smile.
I stand aside and marvel; for a while
The winter sun is pleasant and it warms
My heart with love for others, but the swarms
Of penitents have dwindled. I begin
To cry and ask God's pardon of our sin.
Where are you? You were with me and are gone.
All the forgiven couples hurry on
To dinner and their nights, and none will stop.
I run about in circles till I drop

Against a padlocked bulkhead in a yard
Where faces redden and the snow is hard.

IV.
AT THE ALTAR

I sit at a gold table with my girl
Whose eyelids burn with brandy. What a whirl
Of Easter eggs is colored by the lights,
As the Norwegian dancer's crystalled tights
Flash with her naked leg's high-booted skate,
Like Northern Lights upon my watching plate.
The twinkling steel above me is a star;
I am a fallen Christmas tree. Our car
Races through seven red-lights—then the road
Is unpatrolled and empty, and a load
Of ply-wood with a tail-light makes us slow.
I turn and whisper in her ear. You know
I want to leave my mother and my wife,
You wouldn't have me tied to them for life . . .
Time runs, the windshield runs with stars. The past
Is cities from a train, until at last
Its escalating and black-windowed blocks
Recoil against a Gothic church. The clocks
Are tolling. I am dying. The shocked stones
Are falling like a ton of bricks and bones
That snap and splinter and descend in glass
Before a priest who mumbles through his Mass
And sprinkles holy water; and the Day
Breaks with its lightning on the man of clay,
Dies amara valde. Here the Lord
Is Lucifer in harness: hand on sword,
He watches me for Mother, and will turn
The bier and baby-carriage where I burn.

In the Cage

The lifers file into the hall,
According to their houses—twos
Of laundered denim. On the wall
A colored fairy tinkles blues
And titters by the balustrade;
Canaries beat their bars and scream.
We come from tunnels where the spade
Pick-axe and hod for plaster steam
In mud and insulation. Here
The Bible-twisting Israelite
Fasts for his Harlem. It is night,
And it is vanity, and age
Blackens the heart of Adam. Fear,
The yellow chirper, beaks its cage.

Mr. Edwards and the Spider

I saw the spiders marching through the air,
Swimming from tree to tree that mildewed day
   In latter August when the hay
   Came creaking to the barn. But where
     The wind is westerly,
Where gnarled November makes the spiders fly
Into the apparitions of the sky,
They purpose nothing but their ease and die
Urgently beating east to sunrise and the sea;

What are we in the hands of the great God?
It was in vain you set up thorn and briar
   In battle array against the fire
   And treason crackling in your blood;
     For the wild thorns grow tame
And will do nothing to oppose the flame;
Your lacerations tell the losing game
You play against a sickness past your cure.
How will the hands be strong? How will the heart endure?

A very little thing, a little worm,
Or hourglass-blazoned spider, it is said,
   Can kill a tiger. Will the dead
   Hold up his mirror and affirm
     To the four winds the smell
And flash of his authority? It's well
If God who holds you to the pit of hell,
Much as one holds a spider, will destroy,
Baffle and dissipate your soul. As a small boy

On Windsor Marsh, I saw the spider die
When thrown into the bowels of fierce fire:
 There's no long struggle, no desire
 To get up on its feet and fly—
  It stretches out its feet
And dies. This is the sinner's last retreat;
Yes, and no strength exerted on the heat
Then sinews the abolished will, when sick
And full of burning, it will whistle on a brick.

But who can plumb the sinking of that soul?
Josiah Hawley, picture yourself cast
 Into a brick-kiln where the blast
 Fans your quick vitals to a coal—
  If measured by a glass,
How long would it seem burning! Let there pass
A minute, ten, ten trillion; but the blaze
Is infinite, eternal: this is death,
To die and know it. This is the Black Widow, death.

Where the Rainbow Ends

I saw the sky descending, black and white,
Not blue, on Boston where the winters wore
The skulls to jack-o'-lanterns on the slates,
And Hunger's skin-and-bone retrievers tore
The chickadee and shrike. The thorn tree waits
Its victim and tonight
The worms will eat the deadwood to the foot
Of Ararat: the scythers, Time and Death,
Helmed locusts, move upon the tree of breath;
The wild ingrafted olive and the root

Are withered, and a winter drifts to where
The Pepperpot, ironic rainbow, spans
Charles River and its scales of scorched-earth miles.
I saw my city in the Scales, the pans
Of judgment rising and descending. Piles
Of dead leaves char the air—
And I am a red arrow on this graph
Of Revelations. Every dove is sold
The Chapel's sharp-shinned eagle shifts its hold
On serpent-Time, the rainbow's epitaph.

In Boston serpents whistle at the cold.
The victim climbs the altar steps and sings:
"Hosannah to the lion, lamb, and beast
Who fans the furnace-face of IS with wings:
I breathe the ether of my marriage feast."
At the high altar, gold
And a fair cloth. I kneel and the wings beat

My cheek. What can the dove of Jesus give
You now but wisdom, exile? Stand and live,
The dove has brought an olive branch to eat.

from

The Mills of the Kavanaughs

(1951)

from Her Dead Brother

I.
The Lion of St. Mark's upon the glass
Shield in my window reddens, as the night
Enchants the swinging dories to its terrors,
And dulls your distant wind-stung eyes; alas,
Your portrait, coiled in German-silver hawsers, mirrors
The sunset as a dragon. Enough light
Remains to see you through your varnish. Giving
Your life has brought you closer to your friends;
Yes, it has brought you home. All's well that ends:
Achilles dead is greater than the living;

My mind holds you as I would have you live,
A wintering dragon. Summer was too short
When we went picnicking with telescopes
And crocking leather handbooks to that fort
Above the lank and heroned Sheepscot, where its slopes
Are clutched by hemlocks—spotting birds. I give
You back that idyll, Brother. Was it more?
Remember riding, scotching with your spur
That four-foot milk-snake in a juniper?
Father shellacked it to the ice-house door.

Then you were grown; I left you on your own.
We will forget that August twenty-third,
When Mother motored with the maids to Stowe,
And the pale summer shades were drawn—so low
No one could see us; no, nor catch your hissing word,
As false as Cressid! Let our deaths atone:
The fingers on your sword-knot are alive,

And Hope, that fouls my brightness with its grace,
Will anchor in the narrows of your face.
My husband's Packard crunches up the drive.

from

Life Studies

(1959)

Beyond the Alps

(On the train from Rome to Paris. 1950, the year Pius XII defined the dogma
of Mary's bodily assumption.)

Reading how even the Swiss had thrown the sponge
in once again and Everest was still
unscaled, I watched our Paris pullman lunge
mooning across the fallow Alpine snow.
O bella Roma! I saw our stewards go
forward on tiptoe banging on their gongs.
Life changed to landscape. Much against my will
I left the City of God where it belongs.
There the skirt-mad Mussolini unfurled
the eagle of Caesar. He was one of us
only, pure prose. I envy the conspicuous
waste of our grandparents on their grand tours—
long-haired Victorian sages accepted the universe,
while breezing on their trust funds through the world.

When the Vatican made Mary's Assumption dogma,
the crowds at San Pietro screamed *Papa.*
The Holy Father dropped his shaving glass,
and listened. His electric razor purred,
his pet canary chirped on his left hand.
The lights of science couldn't hold a candle
to Mary risen—at one miraculous stroke,
angel-wing'd, gorgeous as a jungle bird!
But who believed this? Who could understand?
Pilgrims still kissed Saint Peter's brazen sandal.
The Duce's lynched, bare, booted skull still spoke.

God herded his people to the *coup de grâce*—
the costumed Switzers sloped their pikes to push,
O Pius, through the monstrous human crush. . . .

Our mountain-climbing train had come to earth.
Tired of the querulous hush-hush of the wheels,
the blear-eyed ego kicking in my berth
lay still, and saw Apollo plant his heels
on terra firma through the morning's thigh . . .
each backward, wasted Alp, a Parthenon,
fire-branded socket of the Cyclops' eye.
There were no tickets for that altitude
once held by Hellas, when the Goddess stood,
prince, pope, philosopher and golden bough,
pure mind and murder at the scything prow—
Minerva, the miscarriage of the brain.

Now Paris, our black classic, breaking up
like killer kings on an Etruscan cup.

A Mad Negro Soldier Confined at Munich

"We're all Americans, except the Doc,
a Kraut DP, who kneels and bathes my eye.
The boys who floored me, two black maniacs, try
to pat my hands. Rounds, rounds! Why punch the clock?

In Munich the zoo's rubble fumes with cats;
hoydens with air-guns prowl the Koenigsplatz,
and pink the pigeons on the mustard spire.
Who but my girl-friend set the town on fire?

Cat-houses talk cold turkey to my guards;
I found my *Fräulein* stitching outing shirts
in the black forest of the colored wards—
lieutenants squawked like chickens in her skirts.

Her German language made my arteries harden—
I've no annuity from the pay we blew.
I chartered an aluminum canoe,
I had her six times in the English Garden.

Oh mama, mama, like a trolley-pole
sparking at contact, her electric shock—
the power-house! . . . The doctor calls our roll—
no knives, no forks. We file before the clock,

and fancy minnows, slaves of habit, shoot
like starlight through their air-conditioned bowl.
It's time for feeding. Each subnormal boot-
black heart is pulsing to its ant-egg dole."

The account of him is platitudinous, worldly and fond, but he has no Christian name and is entitled merely Major *M*. Myers in my Cousin Cassie Mason Myers Julian-James's privately printed *Biographical Sketches: A Key to a Cabinet of Heirlooms in the Smithsonian Museum*. The name-plate under his portrait used to spell out his name bravely enough: he was Mordecai Myers. The artist painted Major Myers in his sanguine War of 1812 uniform with epaulets, white breeches, and a scarlet frogged waistcoat. His right hand played with the sword "now to be seen in the Smithsonian cabinet of heirlooms." The pose was routine and gallant. The full-lipped smile was good-humoredly pompous and embarrassed.

Mordecai's father, given neither name nor initial, is described with an air of hurried self-congratulation by Cousin Cassie as "a friend of the Reverend Ezra Styles, afterward President of Yale College." As a very young man the son, Mordecai, studied military tactics under a French émigré, "the Bourbons' celebrated Colonel De la Croix." Later he was "matured" by six years' practical experience in a New York militia regiment organized by Colonel Martin Van Buren. After "the successful engagement against the British at Chrysler's Field, thirty shrapnel splinters were extracted from his shoulder." During convalescence, he wooed and won Miss Charlotte Bailey, "thus proving himself a better man than his rivals, the united forces of Plattsburg." He fathered ten children, sponsored an enlightened law exempting Quakers from military service in New York State, and died in 1870 at the age of ninety-four, "a Grand Old Man, who impressed strangers with the poise of his old-time manners."

Undoubtedly Major Mordecai had lived in a more ritualistic, gaudy, and animal world than twentieth-century Boston. There was something undecided, Mediterranean, versatile, almost double-faced about his bearing which suggested that, even to his contemporaries, he must have seemed gratuitously both *ci-devant* and *parvenu*. He was a dark man, a German Jew—no downright Yankee, but maybe such a fellow as Napoleon's mad, pomaded son-of-an-innkeeper general, Junot, Duc D'Abrantes; a man like mad George III's pomaded, disreputable son, "Prinny," the Prince Regent. Or he was one of those Moorish-looking dons painted by his contemporary Goya—some leader of Spanish guerrillas against Bonaparte's occupation, who fled to South America. Our Major's suffering almond eye rested on his luxurious dawn-colored fingers ruffling an off-white glove.

Bailey-Mason-Myers! Easy-going, Empire State patricians, these relatives of my Grandmother Lowell seemed to have given my father his character. For he likewise lacked that granite *back-countriness* which Grandfather Arthur Winslow attributed to his own ancestors, the iconoclastic, mulish Dunbarton New Hampshire Starks. On the joint Mason-Myers bookplate, there are two merry and naked mermaids—lovely, marshmallowy, boneless, Rubensesque butterballs, all burlesque-show bosoms and Flemish smiles. Their motto, *malo frangere quam flectere*, reads "I prefer to bend than to break."

Mordecai Myers was my Grandmother Lowell's grandfather. His life was tame and honorable. He was a leisured squire and merchant, a member of the state legislature, a mayor of Schenectady, a "president" of Kinderhook village. Disappointingly, his famous "blazing brown eye" seems in all things to have shunned the outrageous. After his death he was remembered soberly as a New York State gentleman, the friend and host of worldly men and politicians with Dutch names: De Witt Clinton, Vanderpoel, Hoes, and Schuyler. My mother was roused to warmth by the Major's scarlet vest and exotic eye. She always insisted that he was the one properly dressed and dieted ancestor in the lot we had inherited from my father's Cousin Cassie. Great-great-Grandfather Mordecai! Poor sheepdog in wolf's clothing! In the anarchy of my adolescent war on my parents, I tried to make him a true wolf, the wandering Jew! *Homo lupus homini!*

Major Mordecai Myers' portrait has been mislaid past finding, but out of my memories I often come on it in the setting of our Revere Street house, a setting now fixed in the mind, where it survives all the distortions of fantasy, all the blank befogging of forgetfulness. There, the vast number of remembered *things* remains rocklike. Each is in its place, each has its function, its history, its drama. There, all is preserved by that motherly care that one either ignored or resented in his youth. The things and their owners come back urgent with life and meaning—because finished, they are endurable and perfect.

Cousin Cassie only became a close relation in 1922. In that year she died. After some unpleasantness between Mother and a co-heiress, Helen Bailey, the estate was divided. Mother used to return frozen and thrilled from her property disputes, and I, knowing nothing of the rights and wrongs, would half-perversely confuse Helen Bailey with Helen of Troy and harden my mind against the monotonous *parti pris* of Mother's voice. Shortly after our move to Boston in 1924, a score of unwanted Myers portraits was delivered to our new house on Revere Street. These were later followed by "their dowry"—four moving vans groaning with heavy Edwardian furniture. My father began to receive his first quarterly payments from the Mason-Myers Julian-James Trust Fund, sums "not grand enough to corrupt us," Mother explained, "but sufficient to prevent Daddy from being entirely at the mercy of his salary." The Trust sufficed: our lives became tantalized with possibilities, and my father felt encouraged to take the risk—a small one in those boom years—of resigning from the Navy on the gamble of doubling his income in business.

I was in the third grade and for the first time becoming a little more popular at school. I was afraid Father's leaving the Navy would destroy my standing. I was a churlish, disloyal, romantic boy, and quite without hero worship for my father, whose actuality seemed so inferior to the photographs in uniform he once mailed to us from the Golden Gate. My real *love*, as Mother used to insist to all new visitors, was toy soldiers. For a few months at the flood tide of this infatuation, people were ciphers to me—valueless except as chances for increasing my armies of soldiers. Roger Crosby, a child in the second grade of my Brimmer Street School, had thousands—not mass-produced American stereotypes, but hand-painted solid lead soldiers made to order in Dijon, France. Roger's father had a still more artistic and adult collection; its ranks—each man at least six inches tall—marched in glass cases under the eyes of recognizable replicas of mounted Napoleonic captains: Kléber, Marshal Ney, Murat, King of Naples. One delirious afternoon Mr. Crosby showed me his toys and was perhaps the first grownup to talk to me not as a child but as an equal when he discovered how feverishly I followed his anecdotes on uniforms and the evolution of tactical surprise. Afterwards, full of high thoughts, I ran up to Roger's play room and hoodwinked him into believing that his own soldiers were "ballast turned out by central European sweat-shops." He agreed I was being sweetly generous when I traded twenty-four worthless Jordan Marsh papier-mâché doughboys for whole companies of his gorgeous, imported Old Guards, Second Empire "redlegs," and modern *chasseurs d'Alpine* with sky-blue be-rets. The haul was so huge that I had to take a child's wheelbarrow to Roger's house at the top of Pinckney Street. When I reached home with my last load, Mr. Crosby was talking with my father on our front steps. Roger's soldiers were all returned; I had only the presence of mind to hide a single soldier, a peely-nosed black sepoy wearing a Shriner's fez.

Nothing consoled me for my loss, but I enjoyed being al-lowed to draw Father's blunt dress sword, and I was proud of our Major Mordecai. I used to stand dangerously out in the middle of Revere Street in order to see through our windows and gloat on this portrait's scarlet waistcoat blazing in the bare, Spartan whiteness of our den-parlor. Mordecai Myers lost his glory when

I learned from my father that he was only a "major *pro tem*." On a civilian, even a civilian soldier, the flamboyant waistcoat was stuffy and no more martial than officers' costumes in our elementary school musicals.

In 1924 people still lived in cities. Late that summer, we bought the 91 Revere Street house, looking out on an unbuttoned part of Beacon Hill bounded by the North End slums, though reassuringly only four blocks away from my Grandfather Winslow's brown pillared house at 18 Chestnut Street. In the decades preceding and following the First World War, old Yankee families had upset expectation by regaining this section of the Hill from the vanguards of the lace-curtain Irish. This was bracing news for my parents in that topsy-turvy era when the Republican Party and what were called "people of the right sort" were no longer dominant in city elections. Still, even in the palmy, laissez-faire '20s, Revere Street refused to be a straightforward, immutable residential fact. From one end to the other, houses kept being sanded down, repainted, or abandoned to the flaking of decay. Houses, changing hands, changed their language and nationality. A few doors to our south the householders spoke "Beacon Hill British" or the flat *nay nay* of the Boston Brahmin. The parents of the children a few doors north spoke mostly in Italian.

My mother felt a horrified giddiness about the adventure of our address. She once said, "We are barely perched on the outer rim of the hub of decency." We were less than fifty yards from Louisburg Square, the cynosure of old historic Boston's plain-spoken, cold roast elite—the Hub of the Hub of the Universe. Fifty yards!

As a naval ensign, Father had done postgraduate work at Harvard. He had also done postgraduate work at M.I.T., preferred the purely scientific college, and condescended to both. In 1924, however, his tone began to change; he now began to speak warmly of Harvard as his second alma mater. We went to football games at the Harvard Stadium, and one had the feeling that our lives were now being lived in the brutal, fashionable expectancy of the stadium: we had so many downs, so many minutes, and so many yards to go for a winning touchdown. It was just such a winning financial and social advance that my parents promised themselves would follow Father's resignation from the Navy and his acceptance of a sensible job offered him at the Cambridge branch of Lever Brothers' Soap.

The advance was never to come. Father resigned from the service in 1927, but he never had a civilian *career*; he instead had merely twenty-two years of the civilian *life*. Almost immediately he bought a larger and more stylish house; he sold his ascetic, stove-black Hudson and bought a plump brown Buick; later the Buick was exchanged for a high-toned, as-good-as-new Packard with a custom-designed royal blue and mahogany body. Without drama, his earnings more or less decreased from year to year.

But so long as we were on Revere Street, Father tried to come to terms with it and must have often wondered whether he on the whole liked or disliked the neighborhood's lack of side. He was still at this time rather truculently democratic in what might be described as an upper middle-class, naval, and Masonic fashion. He was a mumbler. His opinions were almost morbidly hesitant, but he considered himself a matter-of-fact man of science and had an unspoiled faith in the superior efficiency of northern nations. He modeled his allegiances and humor on the cockney imperialism of Rudyard Kipling's swearing Tommies, who did their job. Autochthonous Boston snobs, such as the Winslows or members of Mother's reading club, were alarmed by the brassy callousness of our naval visitors, who labeled the Italians they met on Revere Street as "grade-A" and "grade-B wops." The Revere Street "grade-B's" were Sicilian Catholics and peddled crummy second-hand furniture on Cambridge Street, not far from the site of Great-great-Grandfather Charles Lowell's disused West Church, praised in an old family folder as "a haven from the Sodom and Gomorrah of Trinitarian orthodoxy and the tyranny of the letter." Revere Street "grade-A's," good North Italians, sold fancy groceries and Colonial heirlooms in their shops near the Public Garden.

Still other Italians were Father's familiars; they sold him bootleg Scotch and *vino rosso* in teacups.

The outside of our Revere Street house was a flat red brick surface unvaried by the slightest suggestion of purple panes, delicate bay, or triangular window-cornice—a sheer wall formed by the seamless conjunction of four inseparable façades, all of the same commercial and purgatorial design. Though placed in the heart of Old Boston, it was ageless and artless, an epitome of those "leveler" qualities Mother found most grueling about the naval service. 91 Revere Street was mass-produced, *regulation-issue*, and yet struck Boston society as stupidly out of the ordinary, like those white elephants—a mother-of-pearl scout knife or a tea-kettle barometer—which my father used to pick up on sale at an Army-Navy store.

The walls of Father's minute Revere Street den-parlor were bare and white. His bookshelves were bare and white. The den's one adornment was a ten-tube home-assembled battery radio set, whose loudspeaker had the shape and color of a Mexican sombrero. The radio's specialty was getting programs from Australia and New Zealand in the early hours of the morning.

My father's favorite piece of den furniture was his oak and "rhinoceros hide" armchair. It was ostentatiously a masculine, or rather a bachelor's, chair. It had a notched, adjustable back; it was black, cracked, hacked, scratched, splintered, gouged, initialed, gunpowder-charred and tumbler-ringed. It looked like pale tobacco leaves laid on dark tobacco leaves. I doubt if Father, a considerate man, was responsible for any of the marring. The chair dated from his plebe days at the Naval Academy, and had been bought from a shady, shadowy, roaring character, midshipman "Beauty" Burford. Father loved each disfigured inch.

My father had been born two months after his own father's death. At each stage of his life, he was to be forlornly fatherless. He was a deep boy brought up entirely by a mild widowed mother and an intense widowed grandmother. When he was fourteen and a half, he became a deep young midshipman. By the time he graduated from Annapolis, he had a high sense of abstract form, which he beclouded with his humor. He had reached, perhaps, his final mental possibilities. He was deep—not with profundity, but with the dumb depth of one who trusted in statistics and was dubious of personal experience. In his forties, Father's soul went underground: as a civilian he kept his high sense of form, his humor, his accuracy, but this accuracy was henceforth unimportant, recreational, *hors de combat*. His debunking grew myopic; his shyness grew evasive; he argued with a fumbling languor. In the twenty-two years Father lived after he resigned from the Navy, he never again deserted Boston and never became Bostonian. He survived to drift from job to job, to be displaced, to be grimly and literally that old cliché, a fish out of water. He gasped and wheezed with impotent optimism, took on new ideals with each new job, never ingeniously enjoyed his leisure, never even hid his head in the sand.

Mother hated the Navy, hated naval society, naval pay, and the trip-hammer rote of settling and unsettling a house every other year when Father was transferred to a new station or ship. She had been married nine or ten years and still suspected that her husband was savorless, unmasterful, merely considerate. Unmasterful—Father's specialized efficiency lacked utterly the flattering bossiness she so counted on from her father, my Grandfather Winslow. It was not Father's absence on sea-duty that mattered; it was the eroding necessity of moving *with* him, of keeping in step. When he was far away on the Pacific, she had her friends, her parents, a house to herself—Boston! Fully conscious of her uniqueness and normality she basked in the refreshing stimulation of dreams in which she imagined Father as suitably sublimed. She used to describe such a sublime man to me over tea and English muffins. He was Siegfried carried lifeless through the shining air by Brunnhilde to Valhalla, and accompanied by the throb of my Great Aunt Sarah playing his leitmotif in the released manner taught her by the Abbé Liszt. Or Mother's hero dove through the grottoes of the Rhine and slaughtered the homicidal and vulgar dragon coiled about the golden hoard. Mother seemed almost light-headed when she retold the romance of Sarah Bernhardt in *L'Aiglon*, the Eaglet, the weakling! She would speak the word *weakling* with such amused vehemence that I formed a grandiose and false image of L'Aiglon's Father, the *big* Napoleon: he was a strong man who scratched under his paunchy little white vest a torso all hair, muscle, and manliness. Instead of the dreams, Mother now had the insipid fatigue of keeping house. Instead of the *Eagle*, she had a twentieth-century naval commander interested in steam, radio, and "the fellows." To avoid naval yards, steam, and "the fellows," Mother had impulsively bought the squalid, impractical Revere Street house. Her marriage daily forced her to squander her subconsciously hoarded energies.

"*Weelawaugh, we-ee-eeelawaugh, weelawaugh*," shrilled Mother's high voice. "*But-and, but-and, but-and!*" Father's low mumble would drone in answer. Though I couldn't be sure that I had caught the meaning of the words, I followed the sounds as though they were a movie. I felt drenched in my parents' passions.

91 Revere Street was the setting for those arthritic spiritual pains that troubled us for the two years my mother spent in trying to argue my father into resigning from the Navy. When the majestic, hollow boredom of the second year's autumn dwindled to the mean boredom of a second winter, I grew less willing to open my mouth. I bored my parents, they bored me.

"Weelawaugh, we-ee-eelawaugh, weelawaugh!" "But-and, but-and, but-and!"

During the week ends I was at home much of the time. All day I used to look forward to the nights when my bedroom walls would once again vibrate, when I would awake with rapture to the rhythm of my parents arguing, arguing one another to exhaustion. Sometimes, without bathrobe or slippers, I would wriggle out into the cold hall on my belly and ambuscade myself behind the banister. I could often hear actual words. "Yes, yes, yes," Father would mumble. He was "backsliding" and "living in the fool's paradise of habitual retarding and retarded do-nothing inertia." Mother had violently set her heart on the resignation. She was hysterical even in her calm, but like a patient and forbearing strategist, she tried to pretend her neutrality. One night she said with murderous coolness, "Bobby and I are leaving for Papá's." This was an ultimatum to force Father to sign a deed placing the Revere Street house in Mother's name.

I writhed with disappointment on the nights when Mother and Father only lowed harmoniously together like cows, as they criticized Helen Bailey or Admiral De Stahl. Once I heard my mother say, "A *man* must make up his *own* mind. Oh Bob, if you are going to resign, do it *now* so I can at least plan for your son's *survival* and education on a single continent."

About this time I was being sent for my *survival* to Dr. Dane, a Quaker chiropractor with an office on Marlborough Street. Dr. Dane wore an old-fashioned light tan druggist's smock; he smelled like a healthy old-fashioned drugstore. His laboratory was free of intimidating technical equipment, and had only the conservative lay roughness and toughness that was so familiar and disarming to us in my Grandfather Winslow's country study or bedroom. Dr. Dane's rosy hands wrenched my shoulders with tremendous eclat and made me feel a hero; I felt unspeakable joy whenever an awry muscle fell back into serenity. My mother, who had no curiosity or imagination for cranky occultism, trusted Dr. Dane's clean, undrugged manliness—so like home. She believed that chiropractic had cured me of my undiagnosed asthma, which had defeated the expensive specialists.

"A penny for your thoughts, Schopenhauer," my mother would say.

"I am thinking about pennies," I'd answer.

"When *I* was a child I used to love telling Mamá everything I had done," Mother would say.

"But you're not a child," I would answer.

I used to enjoy dawdling and humming "Anchors Aweigh" up Revere Street after a day at school. "Anchors Aweigh," the official Navy song, had originally been the song composed for my father's class. And yet my mind always blanked and seemed to fill with a clammy hollowness when Mother asked prying questions. Like other tongue-tied, difficult children, I dreamed I was a master of cool, stoical repartee. "What have you been doing, Bobby?" Mother would ask. "I haven't," I'd answer. At home I thus saved myself from emotional exhaustion.

At school, however, I was extreme only in my conventional mediocrity, my colorless, distracted manner, which came from restless dreams of being admired. My closest friend was Eric Burckhard, the son of a professor of architecture at Harvard. The Burckhards came from Zurich and were very German, not like Ludendorff, but in the kindly, comical, nineteenth-century manner of Jo's German husband in *Little Men*, or in the manner of the crusading *sturm und drang* liberal scholars in second year German novels. "Eric's mother and father are *both* called Dr. Burckhard," my mother once said, and indeed there was something endearingly repellent about Mrs. Burckhard with her doctor's degree, her long, unstylish skirts, and her dramatic, dulling blond braids. Strangely the Burckhards' sober continental bourgeois house was without golden mean—everything was either hilariously old Swiss or madly modern. The Frau Doctor Burckhard used to serve mid-morning hot chocolate with rosettes of whipped cream, and receive her friends in a long, uncarpeted hall–drawing room with lethal ferns and a yellow beeswaxed hardwood floor shining under a central skylight. On the wall there were large expert photographs of what at a distance appeared to be Mont Blanc—they were in reality views of Frank Lloyd Wright's Japanese hotel.

I admired the Burckhards and felt at home in their house, and these feelings were only intensified when I discovered that my mother was always ill at ease with them. The heartiness, the enlightenment, and the bright, ferny greenhouse atmosphere were too much for her.

Eric and I were too young to care for books or athletics. Neither of our houses had absorbing toys or an elevator to go up and down in. We were inseparable, but I cannot imagine what we talked about. I loved Eric because he was more popular than I and yet absolutely *sui generis* at the Brimmer School. He had a chalk-white face and limp, fine, white-blond hair. He was frail, elbowy, started talking with an enthusiastic Mont Blanc chirp and would flush with bewilderment if interrupted. All the other boys at Brimmer wore little tweed golf suits with knickerbockers, but Eric always arrived in a black suit coat, a Byronic collar, and cuffless gray flannel trousers that almost hid his shoes. The long trousers were replaced on warm days by gray flannel shorts, such as were worn by children still in kindergarten. Eric's unenviable and freakish costumes were too old or too young. He accepted the whims of his parents with a buoyant tranquility that I found unnatural.

My first and terminating quarrel with Eric was my fault. Eventually almost our whole class at Brimmer had whooping cough, but Eric's seizure was like his long trousers—untimely: he was sick a month too early. For a whole month he was in quarantine and forced to play by himself in a removed corner of the Public Garden. He was certainly conspicuous as he skiproped with his Swiss nurse under the out-of-the-way Ether Memorial Fountain far from the pond and the swan boats. His parents had decided that this was an excellent opportunity for Eric to brush up on his German, and so the absoluteness of his quarantine was monstrously exaggerated by the fact that child and nurse spoke no English but only a guttural, British-sounding, Swiss German. Round and round and round the Fountain, he played intensely, frailly, obediently, until I began to tease him. Though motioned away by him, I came close. I had attracted some of the most popular Brimmer School boys. For the first time I had gotten favorable attention from several little girls. I came close. I shouted. Was Eric afraid of girls? I imitated his German. *Ein, zwei, drei, BEER*. I imitated Eric's coughing. "He is afraid he will give you whooping cough if he talks or lets you come nearer," the nurse said in her musical Swiss-English voice. I came nearer. Eric flushed, grew white, bent double with coughing. He began to cry, and had to be led away from the Public Garden. For a whole week I routed Eric from the Garden daily, and for two or three days I was a center of interest. "Come see the Lake Geneva spider monkey!" I would shout. I don't know why I couldn't stop. Eric never told his father, I think, but when he recovered we no longer spoke. The breach was so unspoken and intense that our classmates were actually horrified. They even devised a solemn ritual for our reconciliation. We crossed our hearts, mixed spit, mixed blood. The reconciliation was hollow.

My parents' confidences and quarrels stopped each night at ten or eleven o'clock, when my father would hang up his tuxedo, put on his commander's uniform, and take a trolley back to the naval yard at Charlestown. He had just broken in a new car. Like a chauffeur, he watched this car, a Hudson, with an informed vigilance, always giving its engine hair-trigger little tinkerings of adjustment or friendship, always fearful lest the black body, unbeautiful as his boiled shirts, should lose its outline and gloss. He drove with flawless, almost instrumental, monotony. Mother, nevertheless, was forever encouraging him to walk or take taxis. She would tell him that his legs were growing vestigial from disuse and remind him of the time a jack had slipped and he had broken his leg while shifting a tire. "Alone and at night," she would say, "an amateur driver is unsafe in a car." Father sighed and obeyed—only, putting on a martyred and penny-saving face, he would keep his self-respect by taking the trolley rather than a taxi. Each night he shifted back into his uniform, but his departures from Revere Street were so furtive that several months passed before I realized what was happening—we had *two* houses! Our second house was the residence in the Naval Yard assigned to the third in command. It was large, had its own flagpole, and screen porches on three levels—

yet it was something to be ashamed of. Whatever pomp or distinction its possession might have had for us was destroyed by an eccentric humiliation inflicted on Father by his superior, Admiral De Stahl, the commandant at Charlestown. De Stahl had not been consulted about our buying the 91 Revere Street house. He was outraged, stormed about "flaunting private fortunes in the face of naval tradition," and ordered my father to sleep on bounds at the Yard in the house provided for that purpose.

On our first Revere Street Christmas Eve, the telephone rang in the middle of dinner; it was Admiral De Stahl demanding Father's instant return to the Navy Yard. Soon Father was back in his uniform. In taking leave of my mother and grandparents he was, as was usual with him under pressure, a little evasive and magniloquent. "A woman works from sun to sun," he said, "but a sailor's watch is never done." He compared a naval officer's hours with a doctor's, hinted at surprise maneuvers, and explained away the uncommunicative arrogance of Admiral De Stahl: "The Old Man has to be hush-hush." Later that night, I lay in bed and tried to imagine that my father was leading his engineering force on a surprise maneuver through arctic wastes. A forlorn hope! "Hush-hush, hush-hush," whispered the snowflakes as big as street lamps as they broke on Father—broke and buried. Outside, I heard real people singing carols, shuffling snow off their shoes, opening and shutting doors. I worried at the meaning of a sentence I had heard quoted from the *Boston Evening Transcript*: "On this Christmas Eve, as usual, the whole of Beacon Hill can be expected to become a single old-fashioned open house—the names of mine host the Hill, and her guests will read like the contents of the Social Register." I imagined Beacon Hill changed to the snow queen's palace, as vast as the north pole. My father pressed a cold finger to his lip: "hush-hush," and led his surprise squad of sailors around an altar, but the altar was a tremendous cash register, whose roughened nickel surface was cheaply decorated with trowels, pyramids, and Arabic swirls. A great drawer helplessly chopped back and forth, unable to shut because choked with greenbacks. "Hush-hush!" My father's engineers wound about me with their eye-patches, orange sashes, and curtain-ring earrings, like the Gilbert and Sullivan pirates' chorus. . . . Outside on the streets of Beacon Hill, it was night, it was dismal, it was raining. Something disturbing had befallen the familiar and honorable Salvation Army band; its big drum and accordion were now accompanied by drunken voices howling: *The Old Gray Mare, she ain't what she used to be, when Mary went to milk the cow.* A sound of a bosun's whistle. Women laughing. Someone repeatedly rang our doorbell. I heard my mother talking on the telephone. "Your inebriated sailors have littered my doorstep with the dregs of Scollay Square." There was a gloating panic in her voice that showed she enjoyed the drama of talking to Admiral De Stahl. "Sir," she shrilled, "you have compelled my husband to leave me alone and defenseless on Christmas Eve!" She ran into my bedroom. She hugged me. She said, "Oh Bobby, it's such a comfort to have a man in the house." "I am not a man," I said, "I am a boy."

Boy—at that time this word had private associations for me; it meant weakness, outlawry, and yet was a status to be held onto. Boys were a sideline at my Brimmer School. The eight superior grades were limited to girls. In these grades, moreover, scholarship was made subservient to discipline, as if in contempt of the male's two idols: career and earning power. The school's tone, its *ton*, was a blend of the feminine and the military, a bulky reality governed in turn by stridency, smartness, and steadiness. The girls wore white jumpers, black skirts, stockings, and rectangular low-heeled shoes. An ex–West Pointer had been appointed to teach drill; and, at the moment of my enrollment in Brimmer, our principal, the hitherto staid Miss Manice, was rumored to be showing signs of age and of undermining her position with the school trustees by girlish, quite out of character, rhapsodies on the varsity basketball team, winner of two consecutive championships. The lower four grades, peaceful and lackadaisical, were, on the other hand, almost a separate establishment. Miss Manice regarded these "coeducated" classes with amused carelessness, allowed them to wear their ordinary clothes, and . . . carelessness, however, is incorrect—Miss Manice, in her administration of the lower school, showed the inconsistency and euphoria of a dual personality. Here she mysteriously shed all her Prussianism. She quoted Emerson and Mencken, disparaged the English, threatened to break with the past, and boldly coquetted with the non-military American genius by displaying movies illustrating the careers of Edison and Ford. Favored lower school teachers were permitted to use us as guinea pigs for mildly radical experiments. At Brimmer I *un*-learned writing. The script that I had mastered with much agony at my first school was denounced as illegible: I was taught to print according to the Dalton Plan—to this day, as a result, I have to print even my two middle names and can only really *write* two words: "Robert" and "Lowell." Our instruction was subject to bewildering leaps. The usual fall performance by the Venetian glass-blowers was followed by a tour of the Riverside Press. We heard Rudy Vallee, then heard spirituals sung by the Hampton Institute choir. We studied grammar from a formidable, unreconstructed textbook written by Miss Manice's father. There, I battled with figures of speech and Greek terminology: *Chiasmus*, the arrangement of corresponding words in opposite order; *Brachylogy*, the failure to repeat an element that is supplied in more or less modified form. Then all this pedantry was nullified by the introduction of a new textbook which proposed to lift the face of syntax by using game techniques and drawings.

Physical instruction in the lower school was irregular, spontaneous, and had nothing of that swept and garnished barrack-room camaraderie of the older girls' gymnasium exercises. On the roof of our school building, there was an ugly concrete area that looked as if it had been intended for the top floor of a garage. Here we played tag, drew lines with chalk, and chose up sides for a kind of kids' soccer. On bright spring days, Mr. Newell, a submerged young man from Boston University, took us on botanical hikes through the Arboretum. He had an eye for inessentials—read us Martha Washington's poems at the Old State House, pointed out the roof of Brimmer School from the top of the Customs House, made us count the steps of the Bunker Hill Monument, and one rainy afternoon broke all rules by herding us into the South Boston Aquarium in order to give an unhealthy, eager, little lecture on the sewage-consumption of the conger eel. At last Miss Manice seemed to have gotten wind of Mr. Newell's moods. For an afternoon or two she herself served as his substitute. We were walked briskly past the houses of Parkman and Dana, and assigned themes on the spunk of great persons who had overcome physical handicaps and risen to the top of the ladder. She talked about Elizabeth Barrett, Helen Keller; her pet theory, however, was that "women simply are not the equals of men." I can hear Miss Manice browbeating my white and sheepish father, "How can we stand up to you? Where are our Archimedeses, our Wagners, our Admiral Simses?" Miss Manice adored "Sir Walter Scott's *big bow-wow*," wished "Boston had banned the tubercular novels of the Brontës," and found nothing in the world "so simpatico" as the "strenuous life" lived by President Roosevelt. Yet the extravagant hysteria of Miss Manice's philanthropy meant nothing; Brimmer was entirely a woman's world—*dummkopf*, perhaps, but not in the least Quixotic, Brimmer was ruled by a woman's obvious aims and by her naive pragmatism. The quality of this regime, an extension of my mother's, shone out in full glory at general assemblies or when I sat with a handful of other boys on the bleachers of Brimmer's new Manice Hall. In unison our big girls sang "America"; back and forth our amazons tramped—their brows were wooden, their dress was black and white, and their columns followed standard-bearers holding up an American flag, the white flag of the Commonwealth of Massachusetts, and the green flag of Brimmer. At basketball games against Miss Lee's or Miss Winsor's, it was our upper-school champions who rushed onto the floor, as feline and fateful in their pace as lions. This was our own immediate and daily spectacle; in comparison such masculine displays as trips to battle cruisers commanded by comrades of my father seemed eyewash—the Navy moved in a realm as ghostlike and removed from my life as the elfin acrobatics of Douglas Fairbanks or Peter Pan. I wished I were an older girl. I wrote Santa Claus for a field hockey stick. To be a boy at Brimmer was to be small, denied, and weak.

I was promised an improved future and taken on Sunday afternoon drives through the suburbs to inspect the boys' schools: Rivers, Dexter, Country Day. These expeditions were stratagems designed to give me a chance to know my father; Mother noisily stayed behind and amazed me by pretending that I had forbidden her to embark on "men's work." Father, however, seldom insisted, as he should have, on seeing the headmasters in person, yet he made an astonishing number of friends; his trust begat trust, and something about his silences encouraged junior masters and even school janitors to pour out small talk that was detrimental to rival institutions. At each new school, however, all this gossip was easily refuted, worse still Mother was always ready to cross-examine Father in a manner that showed that she was asking questions for the purpose of giving, not of receiving, instruction; she expressed astonishment that a wishy-washy desire to be everything to everybody had robbed a naval man of any reliable concern for his son's welfare. Mother regarded the suburban schools as "gerrymandered" and middle-class; after Father had completed his round of inspections, she made her own follow-up visits and told Mr. Dexter and Mr. Rivers to their faces that she was looking for a "respectable stop-gap" for her son's "three years between Brimmer and Saint Mark's." Saint Mark's was the boarding school for which I had been enrolled at birth, and was due to enter in 1930. I distrusted change, knew each school since kindergarten had been more constraining and punitive than its predecessor, and believed the suburban country day schools were flimsily disguised fronts for reformatories. With the egotistic, slightly paranoid apprehensions of an only child, I wondered what became of boys graduating from Brimmer's fourth grade, feared the worst—we were darkly imperiled, like some annual bevy of Athenian youths destined for the Minotaur. And to judge from my father, men between the ages of six and sixty did nothing but meet new challenges, take on heavier responsibilities, and lose all freedom to explode. A ray of hope in the far future was my white-haired Grandfather Winslow, whose unchecked commands and demands were always upsetting people for their own good—he was all I could ever want to be: the bad boy, the problem child, the commodore of his household.

When I entered Brimmer I was eight and a half. I was distracted in my studies, assented to whatever I was told, picked my nose whenever no one was watching, and worried our third-grade teacher by organizing creepy little gangs of boys at recess. I was girl-shy. Thick-witted, narcissistic, thuggish, I had the conventional prepuberty character of my age; whenever a girl came near me, my whole person cringed like a sponge wrung dry by a clenching fist. I was less rather than more bookish than most children, but the girl I dreamed about continually had wheel-spoke black and gold eyelashes, double-length page-boy blond hair, a little apron, a bold, blunt face, a saucy, shivery way of talking, and . . . a paper body—she was the girl in John Tenniel's illustrations to *Alice in Wonderland*. The invigorating and symmetrical aplomb of my ideal Alice was soon enriched and nullified by a second face, when my father took me to the movies on the afternoon of one of Mother's headaches. An innocuous child's movie, the bloody, all-male *Beau Geste* had been chosen, but instead my father preferred a nostalgic tour of places he had enjoyed on shore leave. We went to the Majestic Theater where he had first seen Pola Negri—where we too saw Pola Negri, sloppy-haired, slack, yawning, ravaged, unwashed . . . an Anti-Alice.

Our class belles, the Norton twins, Elie and Lindy, fell far short of the Nordic Alice and the foreign Pola. Their prettiness, rather fluffy, freckled, bashful, might have escaped notice if they had been one instead of two, and if their manners had been less goodhumored, entertaining, and reliable. What mattered more than sex, athletics, or studies to us at Brimmer was our popularity; each child had an unwritten class-popularity poll inside his head. Everyone was ranked, and all day each of us mooned profoundly on his place, as it quivered like our blood or a compass needle with a thousand revisions. At nine character is, perhaps, too much *in ovo* for a child to be strongly disliked, but sitting next to Elie Norton, I glanced at her and gulped prestige from her popularity. We were not close at first; then nearness made us closer friends, for Elie had a gracious gift, the gift of gifts, I suppose, in a child: she forgot all about the popularity-rank of the classmate she was talking to. No moron could have seemed so uncritical as this airy, chatty, intelligent child, the belle of our grade. She noticed my habit of cocking my head on one side, shutting my eyes, and driving like a bull through opposition at soccer—wishing to amuse without wounding, she called me Buffalo Bull. At general assembly she would giggle with contented admiration at the upper-school girls in their penal black and white. "What bruisers, what beef-eaters! Dear girls," she would sigh, parroting her sophisticated mother, "we shall all become fodder for the governess classes before graduating from Brimmer." I felt that Elie Norton understood me better than anyone except my playful little Grandmother Winslow.

One morning there was a disaster. The boy behind me, no friend, had been tapping at my elbow for over a minute to catch my attention before I consented to look up and see a great golden puddle spreading toward me from under Elie's chair. I dared not speak, smile, or flicker an eyelash in her direction. She ran bawling from the classroom. Trying to catch every eye, yet avoid commitment, I gave sidelong and involuntary smirks at space. I began to feel manic with superiority to Elie Norton and struggled to swallow down a feeling of goaded hollowness—was I deserting her? Our teacher left us on our honor and ran down the hall. The class milled about in a hesitant hush. The girls blushed. The boys smirked. Miss Manice, the principal, appeared. She wore her whitish-brown dress with darker brown spots. Shimmering in the sunlight and chilling us, she stood mothlike in the middle of the classroom. We rushed to our seats. Miss Manice talked about how there was "nothing laughable about a malaise." She broke off. Her face took on an expression of invidious disgust. She was staring at me. . . . In the absentmindedness of my guilt and excitement, I had taken the nearest chair, the chair that Elie Norton had just left. "Lowell," Miss Manice shrieked, "are you going to soak there all morning like a bump on a log?"

When Elie Norton came back, there was really no break in her friendliness toward me, but there was something caved in, something crippled in the way I stood up to her and tried to answer her disengaged chatter. I thought about her all the time; seldom meeting her eyes now, I felt rich and raw in her nearness. I wanted passionately to stay on at Brimmer, and told my mother a fib one afternoon late in May of my last year. "Miss Manice has begged me to stay on," I said, "and enter the fifth grade." Mother pointed out that there had never been a boy in the fifth grade. Contradicted, I grew excited. "If Miss Manice has begged me to stay," I said, "why can't I stay?" My voice rose, I beat on the floor with my open hands. Bored and bewildered, my mother went upstairs with a headache. "If you won't believe me," I shouted after her, "why don't you telephone Miss Manice or Mrs. Norton?"

Brimmer School was thrown open on sunny March and April afternoons and our teachers took us for strolls on the polite, landscaped walks of the Public Garden. There I'd loiter by the old iron fence and gape longingly across Charles Street at the historic Boston Common, a now largely wrong-side-of-the-tracks park. On the Common there were mossy bronze reliefs of Union soldiers, and a captured German tank filled with smelly wads of newspaper. Everywhere there were grit, litter, gangs of Irish, Negroes, Latins. On Sunday afternoons orators harangued about Sacco and Vanzetti, while others stood about heckling and blocking the sidewalks. Keen young policemen, looking for trouble, lolled on the benches. At nightfall a police lieutenant on horseback inspected the Common. In the Garden, however, there was only Officer Lever, a single white-haired and mustached dignitary, who had once been the doorman at the Union Club. He now looked more like a member of the club. "Lever's a man about town," my Grandfather Winslow would say. "Give him Harris tweeds and a glass of Scotch, and I'd take him for Cousin Herbert." Officer Lever was without thoughts or deeds, but Back Bay and Beacon Hill parents loved him just for being. No one asked this hollow and leonine King Log to be clairvoyant about children.

One day when the saucer magnolias were in bloom, I bloodied Bulldog Binney's nose against the pedestal of George Washington's statue in full view of Commonwealth Avenue; then I bloodied Dopey Dan Parker's nose; then I stood in the center of a sundial tulip bed and pelted a little enemy ring of third-graders with wet fertilizer. Officer Lever was telephoned. Officer Lever telephoned my mother. In the presence of my mother and some thirty nurses and children, I was expelled from the Public Garden. I was such a bad boy, I was told, "that *even* Officer Lever had been forced to put his foot down."

New England winters are long. Sunday mornings are long. Ours were often made tedious by preparations for dinner guests. Mother would start airing at nine. Whenever the air grew so cold that it hurt, she closed the den windows; then we were attacked by sour kitchen odors winding up a clumsily rebuilt dumb-waiter shaft. The windows were again thrown open. We sat in an atmosphere of glacial purity and sacrifice. Our breath puffed whitely. Father and I wore sleeveless cashmere jerseys Mother had bought at Filene's Basement. A do-it-yourself book containing diagrams for the correct carving of roasts lay on the arm of Father's chair. At hand were Big Bill Tilden on tennis, Capablanca on chess, newspaper clippings from Sidney Lenz's bridge column, and a magnificent tome with photographs and some American's nationalist sketch of Sir Thomas Lipton's errors in the Cup Defender races. Father made little progress in these diversions, and yet one of the authors assured him that mastery demanded only willing readers who understood the meaning of English words. Throughout the winter a gray-whiteness glared through the single den window. In the apoplectic brick alley, a fire escape stood out against our sooty plank fence. Father believed that churchgoing was undignified for a naval man; his Sunday mornings were given to useful acts such as lettering his three new galvanized garbage cans: R.T.S. LOWELL—U.S.N.

Our Sunday dinner guests were often naval officers. Naval officers were not Mother's sort; very few people *were* her sort in those days, and that was her trouble—a very authentic, human, and plausible difficulty, which made Mother's life one of much suffering. She did not have the self-assurance for wide human experience; she needed to feel liked, admired, surrounded by the approved and familiar. Her haughtiness and chilliness came from apprehension. She would start talking like a *grande dame* and then stand back rigid and faltering, as if she feared being crushed by her own massively intimidating offensive.

Father's old Annapolis roommate, Commander Billy "Battleship Bilge" Harkness, was a frequent guest at Revere Street and one that always threw Mother off balance. Billy was a rough diamond. He made jokes about his "all-American family tree," and insisted that his name, pronounced H*a*rkness, should be spelled H*e*rkness. He came from Louisville, Kentucky, drank whisky to "renew his Bourbon blood," and still spoke with an accent that sounded— so his colleagues said—"like a bran-fed stallion." Like my father, however, Commander Billy had entered the Naval Academy when he was a boy of fourteen; his Southernisms had been thoroughly rubbed away. He was teased for knowing nothing about race horses, mountaineers, folk ballads, hams, sour mash, tobacco . . . Kentucky Colonels. Though hardly an officer and a gentleman in the old Virginian style, he was an unusual combination of clashing virtues: he had led his class in the sciences and yet was what his superiors called "a *mathmaddition* with the habit of command." He and my father, the youngest men in their class, had often been shipmates. Bilge's executive genius had given color and direction to Father's submissive tenacity. He drank like a fish at parties, but was a total abstainer on duty. With reason Commander Harkness had been voted the man most likely to make a four-star admiral in the class of '07.

Billy called his wife *Jimmy* or *Jeems*, and had a rough friendly way of saying, "Oh, Jimmy's bright as a penny." Mrs. Harkness was an unpleasant rarity: she was the only naval officer's wife we knew who was also a college graduate. She had a flat flapper's figure, and hid her intelligence behind a nervous twitter of vulgarity and toadyism. "Charlotte," she would almost scream at Mother, "is this mirAGE, this MIRacle your *own* dining room!"

Then Mother might smile and answer in a distant, though cosy and amused, voice, "I usually manage to make myself pretty comfortable."

Mother's comfort was chic, romantic, impulsive. If her silver service shone, it shone with hectic perfection to rebuke the functional domesticity of naval wives. She had determined to make her *ambiance* beautiful and luxurious, but wanted neither her beauty nor her luxury unaccompanied. Beauty pursued too exclusively meant artistic fatuity of a kind made farcical by her Aunt Sarah Stark Winslow, a beauty too lofty and original ever to marry, a prima donna on the piano, too high-strung ever to give a public recital. Beauty alone meant the maudlin ignominy of having one's investments managed by interfering relatives. Luxury alone, on the other hand, meant for Mother the "paste and fool's-gold polish" that one met with in the foyer of the new Statler Hotel. She loathed the "undernourishment" of Professor Burckhard's Bauhaus modernism, yet in moments of pique she denounced our pompous Myers mahoganies as "suitable for politicians at the Bellevue Hotel." She kept a middle-of-the-road position, and much admired Italian pottery with its fresh peasant colors and puritanical, clean-cut lines. She was fond of saying, "The French *do* have taste," but spoke with a double-edged irony which implied the French, with no moral standards to support their finish, were really no better than naval yahoos. Mother's beautiful house was dignified by a rich veneer of the useful.

"I have always believed carving to be *the* gentlemanly talent," Mother used to proclaim. Father, faced with this opinion, pored over his book of instructions or read the section on table carving in the Encyclopædia Britannica. Eventually he discovered among the innumerable small, specialized Boston "colleges" an establishment known as a carving school. Each Sunday from then on he would sit silent and erudite before his roast. He blinked, grew white, looked winded, and wiped beads of perspiration from his eyebrows. His purpose was to reproduce stroke by stroke his last carving lesson, and he worked with all the formal rightness and particular error of some shaky experiment in remote control. He enjoyed quiet witticisms at the expense of his carving master—"a philosopher who gave himself all the airs of a Mahan!" He liked to pretend that the carving master had stated that "No two cuts are identical," *ergo*: "each offers original problems for the *executioner*." Guests were appeased by Father's saying, "I am just a plebe at this guillotine. Have a hunk of my roast beef hash."

What angered Father was Mrs. Harkness's voice grown merciless with excitement, as she studied his hewing and hacking. She was sure to say something tactless about how Commander Billy was "a stingy artist at carving who could shave General Washington off the dollar bill."

Nothing could stop Commander Billy, that born carver, from reciting verses:

> *"By carving my way*
> *I lived on my pay;*
> *This* reeward, *though small,*
> *Beats none at all . . .*
>
> *My carving paper-thin*
> *Can make a guinea hin,*
> *All giblets, bones, and skin,*
> *Canteen a party of tin."*

And I, furious for no immediate reason, blurted out, "Mother, how much does Grandfather Winslow have to fork up to pay for Daddy's carving school?"

These Sunday dinners with the Harknesses were always woundingly boisterous affairs. Father, unnaturally outgoing, would lead me forward and say, "Bilge, I want you to meet my first coupon from the bond of matrimony."

Commander Billy would answer, "So this is the range-finder you are raising for future wars!" They would make me salute, stand at attention, stand at ease. "Angel-face," Billy would say to me, "you'll skipper a flivver."

"Jimmy" Harkness, of course, knew that Father was anxiously negotiating with Lever Brothers' Soap, and arranging for his resignation from the service, but nothing could prevent her from proposing time and again her "hens' toast to the drakes." Dragging Mother to her feet, Jimmy would scream, "To Bob and Bilgy's next battleship together!"

What Father and Commander Billy enjoyed talking about most was their class of '07. After dinner, the ladies would retire to the upstairs sitting room. As a special privilege I was allowed to remain at the table with the men. Over and over, they would talk about their ensigns' cruise around the world, escaping the "reeport," gunboating on the upper Yangtze during the Chinese Civil War, keeping sane and sanitary at Guantanamo, patroling the Golfo del Papayo during the two-bit Nicaraguan Revolution, when water to wash in cost a dollar a barrel and was mostly "alkali and wrigglers." There were the class casualties: Holden and Holcomb drowned in a foundered launch off Hampton Roads; "Count" Bowditch, killed by the Moros and famous for his dying words to Commander Harkness: "I'm all right. Get on the job, Bilge."

They would speak about the terrible 1918 influenza epidemic, which had killed more of their classmates than all the skirmishes or even the World War. It was an honor, however, to belong to a class which included "Chips" Carpender, whose destroyer, the

Fanning, was the only British or American warship to force a German submarine to break water and surrender. It was a feather in their caps that three of their classmates, Bellinger, Reade, and another, should have made the first trans-Atlantic seaplane flight. They put their faith in teamwork, and Lindbergh's solo hop to Paris struck them as unprofessional, a newspaper trick. What made Father and Commander Billy mad as hornets was the mare's-nest made of naval administration by "deserving Democrats." Hadn't Secretary of State Bryan ordered their old battlewagon the *Idaho* to sail on a goodwill mission to Switzerland? "Bryan, Bryan, Bryan," Commander Billy would boom, "the pious swab had been told that Lake Geneva had annexed the Adriatic." Another "guy with false gills," Josephus Daniels, "ordained by Divine Providence Secretary of the Navy," had refused to send Father and Billy to the war zone. "You are looking," Billy would declaim, "at martyrs in the famous victory of red tape. Our names are rubric." A man they had to take their hats off to was Theodore Roosevelt; Billy had been one of the lucky ensigns who had helped "escort the redoubtable Teddy to Panama." Perhaps because of his viciously inappropriate nickname, "Bilge," Commander Harkness always spoke with brutal facetiousness against the class *bilgers*, officers whose "services were no longer required by the service." In more Epicurean moods, Bilge would announce that he "meant to accumulate a lot of dough from complacent, well-meaning, although misguided West Point officers gullible enough to bet their shirts on the Army football team."

"Let's have a squint at your *figger* and waterline, Bob," Billy would say. He'd admire Father's trim girth and smile familiarly at his bald spot. "Bob," he'd say, "you've maintained your displacement and silhouette unmodified, except for somewhat thinner top chafing gear."

Commander Billy's drinking was a "pain in the neck." He would take possession of Father's sacred "rhino" armchair, sprawl legs astraddle, make the tried and true framework groan, and crucify Mother by roaring out verbose toasts in what he called "me boozy cockney-h'Irish." He would drink to our cocktail shaker. "'Ere's to the 'older of the Lowelldom nectar," he would bellow. "Hip, hip, hooray for señor Martino, h'our h'old hipmate, 'elpmate, and hhonorary member of '07—h'always h'able to navigate and never says dry." We never got through a visit without one of Billy's "Bottoms up to the 'ead of the Nation. "'Ere 's to herb-garden 'Erb." This was a swaggering dig at Herbert Hoover's notoriously correct, but insular, refusal to "imbibe anything more potent than Bromo-Seltzer" at a war-relief banquet in Brussels. Commander Billy's bulbous, water-on-the-brain forehead would glow and trickle with fury. Thinking on Herbert Hoover and Prohibition, he was unable to contain himself. "What a hick! We haven't been steered by a gentleman of parts since the redoubtable Teddy." He recited *wet* verses, such as the following inserted in Father's class book:

> "*I tread the bridge with measured pace;*
> *Proud, yet anguish marks my face—*
> *What worries me like crushing sin*
> *Is where on the sea can I buy dry gin?*"

In his cups, Commander Bilge acted as though he owned us. He looked like a human ash-heap. Cigar ashes buried the heraldic hedgehog on the ash tray beside him; cigar ashes spilled over and tarnished the golden stork embroidered on the table-cover; cigar ashes littered his own shiny blue-black uniform. Greedily Mother's eyes would brighten, drop and brighten. She would say darkly, "I was brought up by Papà to be like a naval officer, to be ruthlessly neat."

Once Commander Billy sprawled back so recklessly that the armchair began to come apart. "You see, Charlotte," he said to Mother, "at the height of my *climacteric* I am breaking Bob's chair."

Harkness went in for tiresome, tasteless harangues against Amy Lowell, which he seemed to believe necessary for the enjoyment of his after-dinner cigar. He would point a stinking baby stogie at Mother. "'Ave a peteeto cigareeto, Charlotte," he would crow. "Puff on this whacking black cheroot, and you'll be a match for any reeking señorita *femme fatale* in the spiggotty republics, where blindness from Bob's bathtub hooch is still unknown. When you go up in smoke, Charlotte, remember the *Maine*. Remember Amy Lowell, that cigar-chawing, guffawing, senseless and meterless, multimillion-heiress, heavyweight mascot on a floating fortress. Damn the *Patterns!* Full speed ahead on a cigareeto!"

Amy Lowell was never a welcome subject in our household. Of course, no one spoke disrespectfully of Miss Lowell. She had been so plucky, so *formidable, so beautifully and unblushingly immense*, as Henry James might have said. And yet, though irreproachably decent herself apparently, like Mae West she seemed to provoke indecorum in others. There was an anecdote which I was too young to understand: it was about Amy's getting her migraine headaches from being kept awake by the exercises of honeymooners in an adjacent New York hotel room. Amy's relatives would have liked to have honored her as a *personage*, a personage a little *outrée* perhaps, but perfectly within the natural order, like Amy's girlhood idol, the Duse. Or at least she might have been unambiguously tragic, short-lived, and a classic, like her last idol, John Keats. My parents piously made out a case for Miss Lowell's *Life of Keats*, which had killed its author and was so much more manly and intelligible than her poetry. Her poetry! But was *poetry* what one could call Amy's loud, bossy, unladylike *chinoiserie*—her free verse! For those that could understand it, her matter was, no doubt, blameless, but the effrontery of her manner made my parents relish Robert Frost's remark that "writing free verse was like playing tennis without a net."

Whenever Amy Lowell was mentioned Mother bridled. Not distinguishing, not caring whether her relative were praised or criticized, she would say, "Amy had the courage of her convictions. She worked like a horse." Mother would conclude characteristically, "Amy did insist on doing everything the *hard* way. I think, perhaps, that her brother, the President of Harvard, did more for *other* people."

Often Father seemed to pay little attention to the conversation of his guests. He would smack his lips, and beam absentmindedly and sensuously, as if he were anticipating the comforts of civilian life—a perpetual shore leave in Hawaii. The Harknesses, however, cowed him. He would begin to feel out the subject of his resignation and observe in a wheedle obscurely loaded with significance that "certain *cits*, no brighter than you or I, pay income taxes as large as a captain's yearly salary."

Commander Harkness, unfortunately, was inclined to draw improper conclusions from such remarks. Disregarding the "romance of commerce," he would break out into ungentlemanly tirades against capital. "Yiss, old Bob," he would splutter, "when I consider the ungodly hoards garnered in by the insurance and broking gangs, it breaks my heart. Riches, reaches, overreaches! If Bob and I had half the swag that Harkness of Yale has just given Lowell of Harvard to build Georgian houses for Boston quee-eers with British accents!" He rumbled on morosely about retired naval officers "forced to live like coolies on their half-pay. Hurrah for the Bull Moose Party!" he'd shout. "Hurrah for Boss Curley! Hurrah for the Bolshies!"

Nothing prevented Commander Billy from telling about his diplomatic mission in 1918, when "his eyes had seen the Bolshie on his native heath." He had been in Budapest "during the brief sway of Béla Kun-Whon. Béla was giving those Hunkyland money-bags and educators the boot into the arms of American philanthropy!"

Then Mother would say, hopefully, "Mamá always said that the *old* Hungarians *did* have taste. Billy, your reference to Budapest makes me heartsick for Europe. I am dying for Bob and Bobby's permission to spend next summer at Etretat."

Commander Billy Harkness specialized in verses like "The Croix de Guerre":

> *"I toast the guy, who, crossing over,*
> *Abode in London for a year,*
> *The guy who to his wife and lover*

> *Returned with conscience clean and clear,*
> *Who nightly prowling Piccadilly*
> *Gave icy stares to floozies wild,*
> *And when approached said, 'Bilgy Billy*
> *Is mama's darling angel child—'*
> *Now he's the guy who rates the croy dee geer!*"

Mother, however, smiled mildly. "Billy," she would say, "my cousin, Admiral Ledyard Atkinson, always has a twinkle in his eye when he asks after your *vers de société.*"

"'Tommy' Atkins!" snorted Commander Billy. "I know Tommy better than my own mother. He's the first chapter in a book I'm secretly writing and leaving to the archives called *Wild Admirals I Have Known.* And now my bodily presence may no longer grace the inner sanctum of the Somerset Club, for fear Admiral Tommy'll assault me with five new chapters of his *Who Won the Battle of Jutland?*"

After the heat and push of Commander Billy, it was pleasant to sit in the shade of the Atkinsons. Cousin Ledyard wasn't exactly an admiral: he had been promoted to this rank during the World War and had soon reverted back to his old rank of captain. In 1926 he was approaching the retiring age and was still a captain. He was in charge of a big, stately, comfortable, but anomalous warship, which seldom sailed further than hailing distance from its Charlestown drydock. He was himself stately and anomalous. Serene, silver-maned, and Spanish-looking, Cousin Ledyard liked full-dress receptions and crowed like a rooster in his cabin crowded with liveried Filipinos, Cuban trophies, and racks of experimental firearms, such as pepper-box pistols and a machine gun worked by electric batteries. He rattled off Spanish phrases, told first-hand adventure stories about service with Admiral Schley, and reminded one of some landsman and diplomat commanding a galleon in Philip II's Armada. With his wife's money he had bought a motor launch which had a teak deck and a newfangled diesel engine. While his warship perpetually rode at anchor, Cousin Ledyard was forever hurrying about the harbor in his launch. "Oh, Led Atkinson has dash and his own speedboat!" This was about the best my father could bring himself to say for his relative. Commander Billy, himself a man of action, was more sympathetic: "Tommy's about a hundred horse and buggy power." Such a dinosaur, however, had little to offer an '07 Annapolis graduate. Billy's final judgment was that Cousin Ledyard knew less *trig* than a schoolgirl, had been promoted through mistaken identity or merely as "window-dressing," and "was really plotting to put airplane carriers in square sails to stem the tide of our declining Yankee seamanship." Mother lost her enthusiasm for Captain Atkinson's stately chatter—he was "unable to tell one woman from another."

Cousin Ledyard's wife, a Schenectady Hoes distantly related to my still living Great-Grandmother Myers, was twenty years younger than her husband. This made her a trying companion; with the energy of youth she demanded the homage due to age. Once while playing in the Mattapoisett tennis tournament, she had said to her opponent, a woman her own age but married to a young husband, "I believe I'll call you Ruth; you can call me Mrs. Atkinson." She was a radiant Christian Scientist, darted about in smart serge suits and blouses frothing with lace. She filled her purse with Science literature and boasted without irony of "Boston's greatest grand organ" in the Christian Science mother temple on Huntington Avenue. As a girl, she had grown up with our Myers furniture. We dreaded Mrs. Atkinson's descents on Revere Street. She pooh-poohed Mother's taste, snorted at our ignorance of Myers family history, treated us as mere custodians of the Myers furniture, resented alterations, and had the memory of a mastodon for Cousin Cassie's associations with each piece. She wouldn't hear of my mother's distress from neuralgia, dismissed my asthma as "growing-pains," and sought to rally us by gossiping about healers. She talked a prim, sprightly babble. Like many Christian Scientists, she had a bloodless, euphoric, inexhaustible interest in her own body. In a discourse which lasted from her first helping of roast beef through her second demitasse, Mrs. Atkinson held us spellbound by telling how her healer had "surprised and evaporated a cyst inside a sac" inside her "major intestine."

I can hear my father trying to explain his resignation from the Navy to Cousin Ledyard or Commander Billy. Talking with an unnatural and importunate jocularity, he would say, "Billy Boy, it's a darned shame, but this State of Massachusetts doesn't approve of the service using its franchise and voting by mail. I haven't had a chance to establish residence since our graduation in '07. I think I'll put my blues in mothballs and become a *cit* just to prove I still belong to the country. The directors of Lever Brothers' Soap in Cambridge . . . I guess for *cits*, Billy, they've really got something on the ball, because they tell me they want me on their team."

Or Father, Cousin Ledyard, Commander Billy, and I would be sitting on after dinner at the dining-room table and talking man to man. Father would say, "I'm afraid I'll grow dull and drab with all this goldbricking ashore. I am too old for tennis singles, but too young for that confirmed state of senility known as golf."

Cousin Ledyard and Commander Billy would puff silently on their cigars. Then Father would try again and say pitifully, "I don't think a naval man can ever on the *outside* replace the friends he made during his years of wearing the blue."

Then Cousin Ledyard would give Father a polite, funereal look and say, "Speaking of golf, Bob, you've hit me below the belt. I've been flubbing away at the game for thirty years without breaking ninety."

Commander Billy was blunter. He would chaff Father about becoming a "beachcomber" or "purser for the Republican junior chamber of commerce." He would pretend that Father was in danger of being jailed for evading taxes to support "Uncle Sam's circus." *Circus* was Commander Billy's slang for the Navy. The word reminded him of a comparison, and once he stood up from the table and bellowed solemnly: "Oyez, oyez! Bob Lowell, our bright boy, our class baby, is now on a par with 'Rattle-Ass Rats'

Richardson, who resigned from us to become press agent for Sells-Floto Circus, and who writes me: 'Bilgy Dear—Beating the drum ahead of the elephants and the spangled folk, I often wonder why I run into so few of my classmates.'"

Those dinners, those apologies! Perhaps I exaggerate their embarrassment because they hover so grayly in recollection and seem to anticipate ominously my father's downhill progress as a civilian and Bostonian. It was to be expected, I suppose, that Father should be in irons for a year or two, while becoming detached from his old comrades and interests, while waiting for the new life.

I used to sit through the Sunday dinners absorbing cold and anxiety from the table. I imagined myself hemmed in by our new, inherited Victorian Myers furniture. In the bleak Revere Street dining room, none of these pieces had at all that air of unhurried condescension that had been theirs behind the summery veils of tissue paper in Cousin Cassie Julian-James's memorial volume. Here, table, highboy, chairs, and screen—mahogany, cherry, teak—looked nervous and disproportioned. They seemed to wince, touch elbows, shift from foot to foot. High above the highboy, our gold National Eagle stooped forward, plastery and doddering. The Sheffield silver-plate urns, more precious than solid sterling, peeled; the bodies of the heraldic mermaids on the Mason-Myers crest blushed a metallic copper tan. In the harsh New England light, the bronze sphinxes supporting our sideboard looked as though manufactured in Grand Rapids. All too clearly no one had worried about synchronizing the grandfather clock's minutes, days, and months with its mellow old Dutch seascape-painted discs for showing the phases of the moon. The stricken, but still striking gong made sounds like steam banging through pipes. Colonel Myers' monumental Tibetan screen had been impiously shortened to fit it for a low Yankee ceiling. And now, rough and gawky, like some Hindu water buffalo killed in mid-rush but still alive with mad momentum, the screen hulked over us . . . and hid the pantry sink.

Our real blue-ribbon-winning *bête noire* was of course the portrait of Cousin Cassie's father, Mordecai Myers' fourth and most illustrious son: Colonel Theodorus Bailey Myers. The Colonel, like half of our new portraits, was merely a collateral relation; though really as close to us as James Russell Lowell, no one called the Colonel "Great Grand Uncle," and Mother playfully pretended that her mind was overstrained by having to remember his full name, rank, and connection. In the portrait, Colonel Theodorus wore a black coat and gray trousers, an obsequiously conservative costume which one associated with undertakers and the musicians at Symphony Hall. His spats were pearl gray plush with pearl buttons. His mustache might have been modeled on the mustache of a bartender in a Western. The majestic Tibetan screen enclosed him as though he were an ancestor-god from Lhasa, a blasphemous yet bogus attitude. Mr. Myers' colonel's tabs were crudely stitched to a civilian coat; his New York Yacht Club button glowed like a carnation; his vainglorious picture frame was a foot and a half wide. Forever, his right hand hovered over a glass dome that covered a model locomotive. He was vaguely Middle-Eastern and waiting. A lady in Mother's sewing circle had pertly interpreted this portrait as, "King Solomon about to receive the Queen of Sheba's shares in the Boston and Albany Railroad." Gone now was the Colonel's place of honor at Cousin Cassie's Washington mansion; gone was his charming satire on the belles of 1850, entitled *Nothing to Wear*, which had once been quoted "throughout the length and breadth of the land as generally as was Bret Harte's *Heathen Chinee*"; gone was his priceless collection of autographed letters of *all* the Signers of the Declaration of Independence—he had said once, "my letters will be my tombstone." Colonel Theodorus Bailey Myers had never been a New Englander. His family tree reached to no obscure Somersetshire yeoman named Winslowe or Lowle. He had never even, like his father, Mordecai, gloried in a scarlet War of 1812 waistcoat. His portrait was an indifferent example from a dull, bad period. The Colonel's only son had sheepishly changed his name from Mason-Myers to Myers-Mason.

Waiting for dinner to end and for the guests to leave, I used to lean forward on my elbows, support each cheekbone with a thumb, and make my fingers meet in a clumsy Gothic arch across my forehead. I would stare through this arch and try to make life stop. Out in the alley the sun shone irreverently on our three garbage cans lettered: R.T.S. LOWELL—U.S.N. When I shut my eyes to stop the sun, I saw first an orange disc, then a red disc, then the portrait of Major Myers apotheosized, as it were, by the sunlight lighting the blood smear of his scarlet waistcoat. Still there was no *coup de théâtre* about the Major as he looked down on us with his portly young man's face of a comfortable upper New York State patroon and the friend of Robert Livingston and Martin Van Buren. Great-great-Grandfather Myers had never frowned down in judgment on a Salem witch. There was no allegory in his eyes, no *Mayflower*. Instead he looked peacefully at his sideboard, his cut-glass decanters, his cellaret—the worldly bosom of the Mason-Myers mermaid engraved on a silver-plated urn. If he could have spoken, Mordecai would have said, "My children, my blood, accept graciously the loot of your inheritance. We are all dealers in used furniture."

The man who seems in my memory to sit under old Mordecai's portrait is not my father, but Commander Billy—*the* Commander after Father had thrown in his commission. There Billy would sit glowing, perspiring, bragging. Despite his rowdiness, he even then breathed the power that would make him a vice-admiral and hero in World War II. I can hear him boasting in lofty language of how he had stood up for democracy in the day of Lenin and Béla Kun; of how he "practiced the sport of kings" (i.e., commanded a destroyer) and combed the Mediterranean, Adriatic, and Black Seas like gypsies—seldom knowing what admiral he served under or where his next meal or load of fuel oil was coming from.

It always vexed the Commander, however, to think of the strings that had been pulled to have Father transferred from Washington to Boston. He would ask Mother, "Why in God's name should a man with Bob's brilliant cerebellum go and mess up his record by actually *begging* for that impotent field nigger's job of second in command at the defunct Boston Yard!"

I would squirm. I dared not look up because I knew that the Commander abhorred Mother's dominion over my father, thought my asthma, supposedly brought on by the miasmal damp of Washington, a myth, and considered our final flight to Boston a scandal.

My mother, on the other hand, would talk back sharply and explain to Billy that there was nothing second-string about the Boston Yard except its commandant, Admiral De Stahl, who had gone into a frenzy when he learned that my parents, supposed to live at the naval yard, had set themselves up without his permission at 91 Revere Street. The Admiral had *commanded* Father to reside at the yard, but Mother had bravely and stubbornly held on at Revere Street.

"A really great person," she would say, "knows how to be courteous to his superiors."

Then Commander Harkness would throw up his hands in despair and make a long buffoonish speech. "Would you believe it?" he'd say. "De Stahl, the anile slob, would make Bob Lowell sleep seven nights a week and twice on Sundays in that venerable twenty-room pile provided for his third in command at the yard. 'Bobby me boy,' the Man says, 'henceforth I will that you sleep wifeless. You're to push your beauteous mug into me boudoir each night at ten-thirty and each morn at six. And don't mind me laying to alongside the Missus De Stahl,' the old boy squeaks; 'we're just two oldsters as weak as babies. But Robbie Boy,' he says, 'don't let me hear of you hanging on your telephone wire and bending off the ear of that forsaken frau of yours sojourning on Revere Street. I might have to phone you in a hurry, if I should happen to have me stroke.'"

Taking hold of the table with both hands, the Commander tilted his chair backwards and gaped down at me with sorrowing Gargantuan wonder: "I know why Young Bob is an only child."

To Delmore Schwartz
(Cambridge 1946)

We couldn't even keep the furnace lit!
Even when we had disconnected it,
the antiquated
refrigerator gurgled mustard gas
through your mustard-yellow house,
and spoiled our long maneuvered visit
from T. S. Eliot's brother, Henry Ware. . . .

Your stuffed duck craned toward Harvard from my trunk:
its bill was a black whistle, and its brow
was high and thinner than a baby's thumb;
its webs were tough as toenails on its bough.
It was your first kill; you had rushed it home,
pickled in a tin wastebasket of rum—
it looked through us, as if it'd died dead drunk.
You must have propped its eyelids with a nail,
and yet it lived with us and met our stare,
Rabelaisian, lubricious, drugged. And there,
perched on my trunk and typing-table,
it cooled our universal
Angst a moment, Delmore. We drank and eyed
the chicken-hearted shadows of the world.
Underseas fellows, nobly mad,
we talked away our friends. "Let Joyce and Freud,
the Masters of Joy,
be our guests here," you said. The room was filled
with cigarette smoke circling the paranoid,
inert gaze of Coleridge, back
from Malta—his eyes lost in flesh, lips baked and black.
Your tiger kitten, *Oranges*,

cartwheeled for joy in a ball of snarls.
You said:
"We poets in our youth begin in sadness;
thereof in the end come despondency and madness;
Stalin has had two cerebral hemorrhages!"
The Charles
River was turning silver. In the ebb-
light of morning, we stuck
the duck
-'s web-
foot, like a candle, in a quart of gin we'd killed.

Words for Hart Crane

"When the Pulitzers showered on some dope
or screw who flushed our dry mouths out with soap,
few people would consider why I took
to stalking sailors, and scattered Uncle Sam's
phoney gold-plated laurels to the birds.
Because I knew my Whitman like a book,
stranger in America, tell my country: I,
Catullus redivivus, once the rage
of the Village and Paris, used to play my role
of homosexual, wolfing the stray lambs
who hungered by the Place de la Concorde.
My profit was a pocket with a hole.
Who asks for me, the Shelley of my age,
must lay his heart out for my bed and board."

Terminal Days at Beverly Farms

At Beverly Farms, a portly, uncomfortable boulder
bulked in the garden's center—
an irregular Japanese touch.
After his Bourbon "old fashioned," Father,
bronzed, breezy, a shade too ruddy,
swayed as if on deck-duty
under his six pointed star-lantern—
last July's birthday present.
He smiled his oval Lowell smile,
he wore his cream gabardine dinner-jacket,
and indigo cummerbund.
His head was efficient and hairless,
his newly dieted figure was vitally trim.

Father and Mother moved to Beverly Farms
to be a two minute walk from the station,
half an hour by train from the Boston doctors.
They had no sea-view,
but sky-blue tracks of the commuters' railroad shone
like a double-barrelled shotgun
through the scarlet late August sumac,
multiplying like cancer
at their garden's border.

Father had had two coronaries.
He still treasured underhand economies,
but his best friend was his little black *Chevie*,
garaged like a sacrificial steer
with gilded hooves,
yet sensationally sober,

and with less side than an old dancing pump.
The local dealer, a "buccaneer,"
had been bribed a "king's ransom"
to quickly deliver a car without chrome.

Each morning at eight-thirty,
inattentive and beaming,
loaded with his "calc" and "trig" books,
his clipper ship statistics,
and his ivory slide rule,
Father stole off with the *Chevie*
to loaf in the Maritime Museum at Salem.
He called the curator
"the commander of the Swiss Navy."

Father's death was abrupt and unprotesting.
His vision was still twenty-twenty.
After a morning of anxious, repetitive smiling,
his last words to Mother were:
"I feel awful."

Father's Bedroom

In my Father's bedroom:
blue threads as thin
as pen-writing on the bedspread,
blue dots on the curtains,
a blue kimono,
Chinese sandals with blue plush straps.
The broad-planked floor
had a sandpapered neatness.
The clear glass bed-lamp
with a white doily shade
was still raised a few
inches by resting on volume two
of Lafcadio Hearn's
Glimpses of Unfamiliar Japan.
Its warped olive cover
was punished like a rhinoceros hide.
In the flyleaf:
"Robbie from Mother."
Years later in the same hand:
"This book has had hard usage
on the Yangtze River, China.
It was left under an open
porthole in a storm."

For Sale

Poor sheepish plaything,
organized with prodigal animosity,
lived in just a year—
my Father's cottage at Beverly Farms
was on the market the month he died.
Empty, open, intimate,
its town-house furniture
had an on tiptoe air
of waiting for the mover
on the heels of the undertaker.
Ready, afraid
of living alone till eighty,
Mother mooned in a window,
as if she had stayed on a train
one stop past her destination.

Sailing Home from Rapallo

(February 1954)

Your nurse could only speak Italian,
but after twenty minutes I could imagine your final week,
and tears ran down my cheeks. . . .

When I embarked from Italy with my Mother's body,
the whole shoreline of the *Golfo di Genova*
was breaking into fiery flower.
The crazy yellow and azure sea-sleds
blasting like jack-hammers across
the *spumante*-bubbling wake of our liner,
recalled the clashing colors of my Ford.
Mother travelled first-class in the hold;
her *Risorgimento* black and gold casket
was like Napoleon's at the *Invalides*. . . .

While the passengers were tanning
on the Mediterranean in deck-chairs,
our family cemetery in Dunbarton
lay under the White Mountains
in the sub-zero weather.
The graveyard's soil was changing to stone—
so many of its deaths had been midwinter.
Dour and dark against the blinding snowdrifts,
its black brook and fir trunks were as smooth as masts.
A fence of iron spear-hafts
black-bordered its mostly Colonial grave-slates.
The only "unhistoric" soul to come here
was Father, now buried beneath his recent
unweathered pink-veined slice of marble.
Even the Latin of his Lowell motto:

Occasionem cognosce,
seemed too businesslike and pushing here,
where the burning cold illuminated
the hewn inscriptions of Mother's relatives:
twenty or thirty Winslows and Starks.
Frost had given their names a diamond edge. . . .

In the grandiloquent lettering on Mother's coffin,
Lowell had been misspelled *LOVEL.*
The corpse
was wrapped like *panettone* in Italian tinfoil.

Waking in the Blue

The night attendant, a B.U. sophomore,
rouses from the mare's-nest of his drowsy head
propped on *The Meaning of Meaning*.
He catwalks down our corridor.
Azure day
makes my agonized blue window bleaker.
Crows maunder on the petrified fairway.
Absence! My heart grows tense
as though a harpoon were sparring for the kill.
(This is the house for the "mentally ill.")

What use is my sense of humor?
I grin at Stanley, now sunk in his sixties,
once a Harvard all-American fullback,
(if such were possible!)
still hoarding the build of a boy in his twenties,
as he soaks, a ramrod
with the muscle of a seal
in his long tub,
vaguely urinous from the Victorian plumbing.
A kingly granite profile in a crimson golf-cap,
worn all day, all night,
he thinks only of his figure,
of slimming on sherbet and ginger ale—
more cut off from words than a seal.

This is the way day breaks in Bowditch Hall at McLean's;
the hooded night lights bring out "Bobbie,"
Porcellian '29,
a replica of Louis XVI

without the wig—
redolent and roly-poly as a sperm whale,
as he swashbuckles about in his birthday suit
and horses at chairs.
These victorious figures of bravado ossified young.

In between the limits of day,
hours and hours go by under the crew haircuts
and slightly too little nonsensical bachelor twinkle
of the Roman Catholic attendants.
(There are no Mayflower
screwballs in the Catholic Church.)

After a hearty New England breakfast,
I weigh two hundred pounds
this morning. Cock of the walk,
I strut in my turtle-necked French sailor's jersey
before the metal shaving mirrors,
and see the shaky future grow familiar
in the pinched, indigenous faces
of these thoroughbred mental cases,
twice my age and half my weight.
We are all old-timers,
each of us holds a locked razor.

Home After Three Months Away

Gone now the baby's nurse,
a lioness who ruled the roost
and made the Mother cry.
She used to tie
gobbets of porkrind in bowknots of gauze—
three months they hung like soggy toast
on our eight foot magnolia tree,
and helped the English sparrows
weather a Boston winter.

Three months, three months!
Is Richard now himself again?
Dimpled with exaltation,
my daughter holds her levee in the tub.
Our noses rub,
each of us pats a stringy lock of hair—
they tell me nothing's gone.
Though I am forty-one,
not forty now, the time I put away
was child's-play. After thirteen weeks
my child still dabs her cheeks
to start me shaving. When
we dress her in her sky-blue corduroy,
she changes to a boy,
and floats my shaving brush
and washcloth in the flush. . . .
Dearest, I cannot loiter here
in lather like a polar bear.

Recuperating, I neither spin nor toil.
Three stories down below,

a choreman tends our coffin's length of soil,
and seven horizontal tulips blow.
Just twelve months ago,
these flowers were pedigreed
imported Dutchmen; now no one need
distinguish them from weed.
Bushed by the late spring snow,
they cannot meet
another year's snowballing enervation.

I keep no rank nor station.
Cured, I am frizzled, stale and small.

Memories of West Street and Lepke

Only teaching on Tuesdays, book-worming
in pajamas fresh from the washer each morning,
I hog a whole house on Boston's
"hardly passionate Marlborough Street,"
where even the man
scavenging filth in the back alley trash cans,
has two children, a beach wagon, a helpmate,
and is a "young Republican."
I have a nine months' daughter,
young enough to be my granddaughter.
Like the sun she rises in her flame-flamingo infants' wear.

These are the tranquillized *Fifties*,
and I am forty. Ought I to regret my seedtime?
I was a fire-breathing Catholic C.O.,
and made my manic statement,
telling off the state and president, and then
sat waiting sentence in the bull pen
beside a Negro boy with curlicues
of marijuana in his hair.

Given a year,
I walked on the roof of the West Street Jail, a short
enclosure like my school soccer court,
and saw the Hudson River once a day
through sooty clothesline entanglements
and bleaching khaki tenements.
Strolling, I yammered metaphysics with Abramowitz,
a jaundice-yellow ("it's really tan")
and fly-weight pacifist,

so vegetarian,
he wore rope shoes and preferred fallen fruit.
He tried to convert Bioff and Brown,
the Hollywood pimps, to his diet.
Hairy, muscular, suburban,
wearing chocolate double-breasted suits,
they blew their tops and beat him black and blue.

I was so out of things, I'd never heard
of the Jehovah's Witnesses.
"Are you a C.O.?" I asked a fellow jailbird.
"No," he answered, "I'm a J.W."
He taught me the "hospital tuck,"
and pointed out the T-shirted back
of *Murder Incorporated*'s Czar Lepke,
there piling towels on a rack,
or dawdling off to his little segregated cell full
of things forbidden the common man:
a portable radio, a dresser, two toy American
flags tied together with a ribbon of Easter palm.
Flabby, bald, lobotomized,
he drifted in a sheepish calm,
where no agonizing reappraisal
jarred his concentration on the electric chair—
hanging like an oasis in his air
of lost connections. . . .

Man and Wife

Tamed by *Miltown*, we lie on Mother's bed;
the rising sun in war paint dyes us red;
in broad daylight her gilded bed-posts shine,
abandoned, almost Dionysian.
At last the trees are green on Marlborough Street,
blossoms on our magnolia ignite
the morning with their murderous five days' white.
All night I've held your hand,
as if you had
a fourth time faced the kingdom of the mad—
its hackneyed speech, its homicidal eye—
and dragged me home alive. . . . Oh my *Petite*,
clearest of all God's creatures, still all air and nerve:
you were in your twenties, and I,
once hand on glass
and heart in mouth,
outdrank the Rahvs in the heat
of Greenwich Village, fainting at your feet—
too boiled and shy
and poker-faced to make a pass,
while the shrill verve
of your invective scorched the traditional South.

Now twelve years later, you turn your back.
Sleepless, you hold
your pillow to your hollows like a child;
your old-fashioned tirade—
loving, rapid, merciless—
breaks like the Atlantic Ocean on my head.

"To Speak of the Woe That Is in Marriage"

"It is the future generation that presses into being by means of these exuberant
feelings and supersensible soap bubbles of ours."   —SCHOPENHAUER

"The hot night makes us keep our bedroom windows open.
Our magnolia blossoms. Life begins to happen.
My hopped up husband drops his home disputes,
and hits the streets to cruise for prostitutes,
free-lancing out along the razor's edge.
This screwball might kill his wife, then take the pledge.
Oh the monotonous meanness of his lust. . . .
It's the injustice . . . he is so unjust—
whiskey-blind, swaggering home at five.
My only thought is how to keep alive.
What makes him tick? Each night now I tie
ten dollars and his car key to my thigh. . . .
Gored by the climacteric of his want,
he stalls above me like an elephant."

Skunk Hour

(FOR ELIZABETH BISHOP)

Nautilus Island's hermit
heiress still lives through winter in her Spartan cottage;
her sheep still graze above the sea.
Her son's a bishop. Her farmer
is first selectman in our village;
she's in her dotage.

Thirsting for
the hierarchic privacy
of Queen Victoria's century,
she buys up all
the eyesores facing her shore,
and lets them fall.

The season's ill—
we've lost our summer millionaire,
who seemed to leap from an L. L. Bean
catalogue. His nine-knot yawl
was auctioned off to lobstermen.
A red fox stain covers Blue Hill.

And now our fairy
decorator brightens his shop for fall;
his fishnet's filled with orange cork,
orange, his cobbler's bench and awl;
there is no money in his work,
he'd rather marry.

One dark night,
my Tudor Ford climbed the hill's skull;

I watched for love-cars. Lights turned down,
they lay together, hull to hull,
where the graveyard shelves on the town. . . .
My mind's not right.

A car radio bleats,
"Love, O careless Love. . . ." I hear
my ill-spirit sob in each blood cell,
as if my hand were at its throat. . . .
I myself am hell;
nobody's here——

only skunks, that search
in the moonlight for a bite to eat.
They march on their soles up Main Street:
white stripes, moonstruck eyes' red fire
under the chalk-dry and spar spire
of the Trinitarian Church.

I stand on top
of our back steps and breathe the rich air——
a mother skunk with her column of kittens swills the garbage pail.
She jabs her wedge-head in a cup
of sour cream, drops her ostrich tail,
and will not scare.

from

Imitations

(1961)

The Infinite

That hill pushed off by itself was always dear
to me and the hedges near
it that cut away so much of the final horizon.
When I would sit there lost in deliberation,
I reasoned most on the interminable spaces
beyond all hills, on their antediluvian resignation
and silence that passes
beyond man's possibility.
Here for a little while my heart is quiet inside me;
and when the wind lifts roughing through the trees,
I set about comparing my silence to those voices,
and I think about the eternal, the dead seasons,
things here at hand and alive,
and all their reasons and choices.
It's sweet to destroy my mind
and go down
and wreck in this sea where I drown.

                                    Leopardi: *L'infinito.*

The Poet at Seven

When the timeless, daily, tedious affair
was over, his Mother shut
her Bible; her nose was in the air;
from her summit
of righteousness, she could not see the boy:
his lumpy forehead knotted
with turmoil, his soul returned to its vomit.

All day he would sweat obedience.
He was very intelligent, but wrung,
and every now and then a sudden jerk
showed dark hypocrisies at work.
He would clap his hands on his rump,
and strut where the gloom of the hallway rotted
the hot curtains. He stuck out his tongue,
clenched his eyes shut, and saw dots.
A terrace gave on the twilight;
one used to see him up there in the lamplight,
sulking on the railing
under an abyss of air
which hung from the roof. His worst block
was the stultifying slump
of mid-summer—he would lock
himself up in the toilet and inhale
its freshness; there he could breathe.

When winter snowed under the breath of flowers,
and the moon blanched the little bower
behind the house, he would crawl
to the foot of the wall
and lie with his eyeballs squeezed to his arm,

dreaming of some dark revelation,
or listening to the legions of termites swarm
in the horny espaliers. As for compassion,
the only children he could speak to
were creepy, abstracted boys, who hid
match-stick thin fingers yellow and black with mud
under rags stuck with diarrhea.
Their dull eyes drooled on their dull cheeks,
they spoke with the selflessness of morons.
His Mother was terrified,
she thought they were losing caste. This was good—
she had the true blue look that lied.

At seven he was making novels
about life in the Sahara,
where ravished Liberty had fled—
sunrises, buffaloes, jungle, savannahs!
For his facts, he used illustrated weeklies,
and blushed at the rotogravures of naked, red
Hawaiian girls dancing.
A little eight year old tomboy,
the daughter of the next door workers,
came, brown-eyed, terrible,
in a print dress. Brutal and in the know,
she would jump on his back,
and ride him like a buffalo,
and shake out her hair.
Wallowing below
her once, he bit her crotch—
she never wore bloomers—
kicked and scratched, he carried back
the taste of her buttocks to his bedroom.

What he feared most
were the sticky, lost December Sundays,
when he used to stand with his hair gummed back

at a little mahogony stand, and hold
a Bible pocked with cabbage-green mould.
Each night in his alcove, he had dreams.
He despised God, the National Guard,
and the triple drum-beat
of the town-crier calling up the conscripts.
He loved the swearing
workers, when they crowded back, black
in the theatrical twilight to their wards.
He felt clean
when he filled his lungs with the smell—
half hay fever, half iodine—
of the wheat,
he watched its pubic golden tassels swell
and steam in the heat,
then sink back calm.

What he liked best were dark things:
the acrid, dank rings
on the ceiling, and the high,
bluish plaster, as bald as the sky
in his bare bedroom, where he could close
the shutters and lose
his world for hundreds of hours,
mooning doggedly
over his novel, endlessly
expanding with jaundiced skies,
drowned vegetation, and carnations
that flashed like raw flesh
in the underwater green
of the jungle starred with flowers—
dizziness, mania, revulsions, pity!
Often the town playground
below him grew loud with children;
the wind brought him their voices,

and he lay alone on pieces of unbleached canvas,
violently breaking into sail.

                                     Rimbaud: *Les poètes de sept ans.*

Pigeons

(FOR HANNAH ARENDT)

The same old flights, the same old homecomings,
dozens of each per day,
but at last the pigeon gets clear of the pigeon-house . . .
What is home, but a feeling of homesickness
for the flight's lost moment of fluttering terror?

Back in the dovecote, there's another bird,
by all odds the most beautiful,
one that never flew out, and can know nothing of gentleness . . .
Still, only by suffering the rat-race in the arena
can the heart learn to beat.

Think of Leonidas perhaps and the hoplites,
glittering with liberation,
as they combed one another's golden Botticellian hair
at Thermopylae, friends and lovers, the bride and the bridegroom—
and moved into position to die.

Over non-existence arches the all-being—
thence the ball thrown almost out of bounds
stings the hand with the momentum of its drop—
body and gravity,
miraculously multiplied by its mania to return.

Rilke: *Die Tauben.*

from

For the Union Dead

(1964)

Water

It was a Maine lobster town—
each morning boatloads of hands
pushed off for granite
quarries on the islands,

and left dozens of bleak
white frame houses stuck
like oyster shells
on a hill of rock,

and below us, the sea lapped
the raw little match-stick
mazes of a weir,
where the fish for bait were trapped.

Remember? We sat on a slab of rock.
From this distance in time,
it seems the color
of iris, rotting and turning purpler,

but it was only
the usual gray rock
turning the usual green
when drenched by the sea.

The sea drenched the rock
at our feet all day,
and kept tearing away
flake after flake.

One night you dreamed
you were a mermaid clinging to a wharf-pile,
and trying to pull
off the barnacles with your hands.

We wished our two souls
might return like gulls
to the rock. In the end,
the water was too cold for us.

Fall 1961

Back and forth, back and forth
goes the tock, tock, tock
of the orange, bland, ambassadorial
face of the moon
on the grandfather clock.

All autumn, the chafe and jar
of nuclear war;
we have talked our extinction to death.
I swim like a minnow
behind my studio window.

Our end drifts nearer,
the moon lifts,
radiant with terror.
The state
is a diver under a glass bell.

A father's no shield
for his child.
We are like a lot of wild
spiders crying together,
but without tears.

Nature holds up a mirror.
One swallow makes a summer.
It's easy to tick
off the minutes,
but the clockhands stick.

Back and forth!
Back and forth, back and forth—
my one point of rest
is the orange and black
oriole's swinging nest!

The Lesson

No longer to lie reading *Tess of the d'Urbervilles*,
while the high, mysterious squirrels
rain small green branches on our sleep!

All that landscape, one likes to think it died
or slept with us, that we ourselves died
or slept then in the age and second of our habitation.

The green leaf cushions the same dry footprint,
or the child's boat luffs in the same dry chop,
and we are where we were. We were!

Perhaps the trees stopped growing in summer amnesia;
their day that gave them veins is rooted down—
and the nights? They are for sleeping now as then.

Ah the light lights the window of my young night,
and you never turn off the light,
while the books lie in the library, and go on reading.

The barberry berry sticks on the small hedge,
cold slits the same crease in the finger,
the same thorn hurts. The leaf repeats the lesson.

Those Before Us

They are all outline, uniformly gray,
unregenerate arrowheads sloughed up by the path here,
or in the corners of the eye, they play
their thankless, fill-in roles. They never were.

Wormwood on the veranda! Plodding needles
still prod the coarse pink yarn into a dress.
The muskrat that took a slice of your thumb still huddles,
a mop of hair and a heart-beat on the porch—

there's the tin wastebasket where it learned to wait
for us playing dead, the slats it mashed in terror,
its spoor of cornflakes, and the packing crate
it furiously slashed to matchwood to escape.

Their chairs were *ex cathedra*, yet if you draw back the blinds,
(as full of windows as a fishnet now)
you will hear them conspiring, slapping hands
across the bent card-table, still leaf-green.

Vacations, stagnant growth. But in the silence,
some one lets out his belt to breathe, some one
roams in negligee. Bless the confidence
of their sitting unguarded there in stocking feet.

Sands drop from the hour-glass waist and swallow-tail.
We follow their gunshy shadows down the trail—
those before us! Pardon them for existing.
We have stopped watching them. They have stopped watching.

Eye and Tooth

My whole eye was sunset red,
the old cut cornea throbbed,
I saw things darkly,
as through an unwashed goldfish globe.

I lay all day on my bed.
I chain-smoked through the night,
learning to flinch
at the flash of the matchlight.

Outside, the summer rain,
a simmer of rot and renewal,
fell in pinpricks.
Even new life is fuel.

My eyes throb.
Nothing can dislodge
the house with my first tooth
noosed in a knot to the doorknob.

Nothing can dislodge
the triangular blotch
of rot on the red roof,
a cedar hedge, or the shade of a hedge.

No ease from the eye
of the sharp-shinned hawk in the birdbook there,
with reddish brown buffalo hair
on its shanks, one ascetic talon

clasping the abstract imperial sky.
It says:
an eye for an eye,
a tooth for a tooth.

No ease for the boy at the keyhole,
his telescope,
when the women's white bodies flashed
in the bathroom. Young, my eyes began to fail.

Nothing! No oil
for the eye, nothing to pour
on those waters or flames.
I am tired. Everyone's tired of my turmoil.

The Public Garden

Burnished, burned-out, still burning as the year
you lead me to our stamping ground.
The city and its cruising cars surround
the Public Garden. All's alive—
the children crowding home from school at five,
punting a football in the bricky air,
the sailors and their pick-ups under trees
with Latin labels. And the jaded flock
of swanboats paddles to its dock.
The park is drying.
Dead leaves thicken to a ball
inside the basin of a fountain, where
the heads of four stone lions stare
and suck on empty faucets. Night
deepens. From the arched bridge, we see
the shedding park-bound mallards, how they keep
circling and diving in the lanternlight,
searching for something hidden in the muck.
And now the moon, earth's friend, that cared so much
for us, and cared so little, comes again—
always a stranger! As we walk,
it lies like chalk
over the waters. Everything's aground.
Remember summer? Bubbles filled
the fountain, and we splashed. We drowned
in Eden, while Jehovah's grass-green lyre
was rustling all about us in the leaves
that gurgled by us, turning upside down . . .
The fountain's failing waters flash around
the garden. Nothing catches fire.

Jonathan Edwards in Western Massachusetts

Edwards' great millstone and rock
of hope has crumbled, but the square
white houses of his flock
stand in the open air,

out in the cold,
like sheep outside the fold.
Hope lives in doubt.
Faith is trying to do without

faith. In western Massachusetts,
I could almost feel the frontier
crack and disappear.
Edwards thought the world would end there.

We know how the world will end,
but where is paradise, each day farther
from the Pilgrim's blues for England
and the Promised Land.

Was it some country house
that seemed as if it were
Whitehall, if the Lord were there?
so nobly did he live.

Gardens designed
that the breath of flowers in the wind,
or crushed underfoot,
came and went like warbling music?

Bacon's great oak grove
he refused to sell,
when he fell,
saying, "Why should I sell my feathers?"

Ah paradise! Edwards,
I would be afraid
to meet you there as a shade.
We move in different circles.

As a boy, you built a booth
in a swamp for prayer;
lying on your back,
you saw the spiders fly,

basking at their ease,
swimming from tree to tree—
so high, they seemed tacked to the sky.
You knew they would die.

Poor country Berkeley at Yale,
you saw the world was soul,
the soul of God! The soul
of Sarah Pierrepont!

So filled with delight in the Great Being,
she hardly cared for anything—
walking the fields, sweetly singing,
conversing with some one invisible.

Then God's love shone in sun, moon and stars,
on earth, in the waters,
in the air, in the loose winds,
which used to greatly fix your mind.

Often she saw you come home from a ride
or a walk, your coat dotted with thoughts
you had pinned there
on slips of paper.

You gave
her Pompey, a Negro slave,
and eleven children.
Yet people were spiders

in your moment of glory,
at the Great Awakening—"Alas, how many
in this very meeting house are more than likely
to remember my discourse in hell!"

The meeting house remembered!
You stood on stilts in the air,
but you fell from your parish.
"All rising is by a winding stair."

On my pilgrimage to Northampton,
I found no relic,
except the round slice of an oak
you are said to have planted.

It was flesh-colored, new,
and a common piece of kindling,
only fit for burning.
You too must have been green once.

White wig and black coat,
all cut from one cloth,
and designed
like your mind!

I love you faded,
old, exiled and afraid
to leave your last flock, a dozen
Housatonic Indian children;

afraid to leave
all your writing, writing, writing,
denying the Freedom of the Will.
You were afraid to be president

of Princeton, and wrote:
"My deffects are well known;
I have a constitution
peculiarly unhappy:

flaccid solids,
vapid, sizzy, scarse fluids,
causing a childish weakness,
a low tide of spirits.

I am contemptible,
stiff and dull.

Why should I leave behind
my delight and entertainment,
those studies
that have swallowed up my mind?"

Caligula

My namesake, Little Boots, Caligula,
you disappoint me. Tell me what I saw
to make me like you when we met at school?
I took your name—poor odd-ball, poor spoiled fool,
my prince, young innocent and bowdlerized!
Your true face sneers at me, mean, thin, agonized,
the rusty Roman medal where I see
my lowest depths of possibility.

What can be salvaged from your life? A pain
that gently darkens over heart and brain,
a fairy's touch, a cobweb's weight of pain,
now makes me tremble at your right to live.
I live your last night. Sleepless fugitive,
your purple bedclothes and imperial eagle
grow so familiar they are home. Your regal
hand accepts my hand. You bend my wrist,
and tear the tendons with your strangler's twist . . .
You stare down hallways, mile on stoney mile,
where statues of the gods return your smile.
Why did you smash their heads and give them yours?
You hear your household panting on all fours,
and itemize your features—sleep's old aide!
Item: your body hairy, badly made,
head hairless, smoother than your marble head;
Item: eyes hollow, hollow temples, red
cheeks rough with rouge, legs spindly, hands that leave
a clammy snail's trail on your soggy sleeve . . .
a hand no hand will hold . . . nose thin, thin neck—
you wish the Romans had a single neck!

Small thing, where are you? Child, you sucked your thumb,
and could not sleep unless you hugged the numb
and wooly-witted toys of your small zoo.
There was some reason then to fondle you
before you found the death-mask for your play.
Lie very still, sleep with clasped hands, and pray
for nothing, Child! Think, even at the end,
good dreams were faithful. You betray no friend
now that no animal will share your bed.
Don't think! . . . And yet the God Adonis bled
and lay beside you, forcing you to strip.
You felt his gored thigh spurting on your hip.
Your mind burned, you were God, a thousand plans
ran zig-zag, zig-zag. You began to dance
for joy, and called your menials to arrange
deaths for the gods. You worshipped your great change,
took a cold bath, and rolled your genitals
until they shrank to marbles . . .

                    Animals
fattened for your arena suffered less
than you in dying—yours the lawlessness
of something simple that has lost its law,
my namesake, and the last Caligula.

July in Washington

The stiff spokes of this wheel
touch the sore spots of the earth.

On the Potomac, swan-white
power launches keep breasting the sulphurous wave.

Otters slide and dive and slick back their hair,
raccoons clean their meat in the creek.

On the circles, green statues ride like South American
liberators above the breeding vegetation—

prongs and spearheads of some equatorial
backland that will inherit the globe.

The elect, the elected . . . they come here bright as dimes,
and die dishevelled and soft.

We cannot name their names, or number their dates—
circle on circle, like rings on a tree—

but we wish the river had another shore,
some further range of delectable mountains,

distant hills powdered blue as a girl's eyelid.
It seems the least little shove would land us there,

that only the slightest repugnance of our bodies
we no longer control could drag us back.

Soft Wood

(FOR HARRIET WINSLOW)

Sometimes I have supposed seals
must live as long as the Scholar Gypsy.
Even in their barred pond at the zoo they are happy,
and no sunflower turns
more delicately to the sun
without a wincing of the will.

Here too in Maine things bend to the wind forever.
After two years away, one must get used
to the painted soft wood staying bright and clean,
to the air blasting an all-white wall whiter,
as it blows through curtain and screen
touched with salt and evergreen.

The green juniper berry spills crystal-clear gin,
and even the hot water in the bathtub
is more than water,
and rich with the scouring effervescence
of something healing,
the illimitable salt.

Things last, but sometimes for days here
only children seem fit to handle children,
and there is no utility or inspiration
in the wind smashing without direction.
The fresh paint
on the captains' houses hides softer wood.

Their square-riggers used to whiten
the four corners of the globe,

but it's no consolation to know
the possessors seldom outlast the possessions,
once warped and mothered by their touch.
Shed skin will never fit another wearer.

Yet the seal pack will bark past my window
summer after summer.
This is the season
when our friends may and will die daily.
Surely the lives of the old
are briefer than the young.

Harriet Winslow, who owned this house,
was more to me than my mother.
I think of you far off in Washington,
breathing in the heat wave
and air-conditioning, knowing
each drug that numbs alerts another nerve to pain.

For the Union Dead

"Relinquunt Omnia Servare Rem Publicam."

The old South Boston Aquarium stands
in a Sahara of snow now. Its broken windows are boarded.
The bronze weathervane cod has lost half its scales.
The airy tanks are dry.

Once my nose crawled like a snail on the glass;
my hand tingled
to burst the bubbles
drifting from the noses of the cowed, compliant fish.

My hand draws back. I often sigh still
for the dark downward and vegetating kingdom
of the fish and reptile. One morning last March,
I pressed against the new barbed and galvanized

fence on the Boston Common. Behind their cage,
yellow dinosaur steamshovels were grunting
as they cropped up tons of mush and grass
to gouge their underworld garage.

Parking spaces luxuriate like civic
sandpiles in the heart of Boston.
A girdle of orange, Puritan-pumpkin colored girders
braces the tingling Statehouse,

shaking over the excavations, as it faces Colonel Shaw
and his bell-cheeked Negro infantry
on St. Gaudens' shaking Civil War relief,
propped by a plank splint against the garage's earthquake.

Two months after marching through Boston,
half the regiment was dead;
at the dedication,
William James could almost hear the bronze Negroes breathe.

Their monument sticks like a fishbone
in the city's throat.
Its Colonel is as lean
as a compass-needle.

He has an angry wrenlike vigilance,
a greyhound's gentle tautness;
he seems to wince at pleasure,
and suffocate for privacy.

He is out of bounds now. He rejoices in man's lovely,
peculiar power to choose life and die—
when he leads his black soldiers to death,
he cannot bend his back.

On a thousand small town New England greens,
the old white churches hold their air
of sparse, sincere rebellion; frayed flags
quilt the graveyards of the Grand Army of the Republic.

The stone statues of the abstract Union Soldier
grow slimmer and younger each year—
wasp-waisted, they doze over muskets
and muse through their sideburns . . .

Shaw's father wanted no monument
except the ditch,
where his son's body was thrown
and lost with his "niggers."

The ditch is nearer.
There are no statues for the last war here;
on Boylston Street, a commercial photograph
shows Hiroshima boiling

over a Mosler Safe, the "Rock of Ages"
that survived the blast. Space is nearer.
When I crouch to my television set,
the drained faces of Negro school-children rise like balloons.

Colonel Shaw
is riding on his bubble,
he waits
for the blessed break.

The Aquarium is gone. Everywhere,
giant finned cars nose forward like fish;
a savage servility
slides by on grease.

from

Near the Ocean

(1967)

Near the Ocean

1. WAKING EARLY SUNDAY MORNING

O to break loose, like the chinook
salmon jumping and falling back,
nosing up to the impossible
stone and bone-crushing waterfall—
raw-jawed, weak-fleshed there, stopped by ten
steps of the roaring ladder, and then
to clear the top on the last try,
alive enough to spawn and die.

Stop, back off. The salmon breaks
water, and now my body wakes
to feel the unpolluted joy
and criminal leisure of a boy—
no rainbow smashing a dry fly
in the white run is free as I,
here squatting like a dragon on
time's hoard before the day's begun!

Vermin run for their unstopped holes;
in some dark nook a fieldmouse rolls
a marble, hours on end, then stops;
the termite in the woodwork sleeps—
listen, the creatures of the night
obsessive, casual, sure of foot,
go on grinding, while the sun's
daily remorseful blackout dawns.

Fierce, fireless mind, running downhill.
Look up and see the harbor fill:

business as usual in eclipse
goes down to the sea in ships—
wake of refuse, dacron rope,
bound for Bermuda or Good Hope,
all bright before the morning watch
the wine-dark hulls of yawl and ketch.

I watch a glass of water wet
with a fine fuzz of icy sweat,
silvery colors touched with sky,
serene in their neutrality—
yet if I shift, or change my mood,
I see some object made of wood,
background behind it of brown grain,
to darken it, but not to stain.

O that the spirit could remain
tinged but untarnished by its strain!
Better dressed and stacking birch,
or lost with the Faithful at Church—
anywhere, but somewhere else!
And now the new electric bells,
clearly chiming, "Faith of our fathers,"
and now the congregation gathers.

O Bible chopped and crucified
in hymns we hear but do not read,
none of the milder subtleties
of grace or art will sweeten these
stiff quatrains shovelled out four-square—
they sing of peace, and preach despair;
yet they gave darkness some control,
and left a loophole for the soul.

No, put old clothes on, and explore
the corners of the woodshed for
its dregs and dreck: tools with no handle,
ten candle-ends not worth a candle,
old lumber banished from the Temple,
damned by Paul's precept and example,
cast from the kingdom, banned in Israel,
the wordless sign, the tinkling cymbal.

When will we see Him face to face?
Each day, He shines through darker glass.
In this small town where everything
is known, I see His vanishing
emblems, His white spire and flag-
pole sticking out above the fog,
like old white china doorknobs, sad,
slight, useless things to calm the mad.

Hammering military splendor,
top-heavy Goliath in full armor—
little redemption in the mass
liquidations of their brass,
elephant and phalanx moving
with the times and still improving,
when that kingdom hit the crash:
a million foreskins stacked like trash . . .

Sing softer! But what if a new
diminuendo brings no true
tenderness, only restlessness,
excess, the hunger for success,
sanity of self-deception
fixed and kicked by reckless caution,
while we listen to the bells—
anywhere, but somewhere else!

O to break loose. All life's grandeur
is something with a girl in summer . . .
elated as the President
girdled by his establishment
this Sunday morning, free to chaff
his own thoughts with his bear-cuffed staff,
swimming nude, unbuttoned, sick
of his ghost-written rhetoric!

No weekends for the gods now. Wars
flicker, earth licks its open sores,
fresh breakage, fresh promotions, chance
assassinations, no advance.
Only man thinning out his kind
sounds through the Sabbath noon, the blind
swipe of the pruner and his knife
busy about the tree of life . . .

Pity the planet, all joy gone
from this sweet volcanic cone;
peace to our children when they fall
in small war on the heels of small
war—until the end of time
to police the earth, a ghost
orbiting forever lost
in our monotonous sublime.

from Brunetto Latini

(Canto XV of Dante's "Inferno")

(FOR LILLIAN HELLMAN)

               ... "Oh, Oh,"
I answered groaning, as I stretched my hand
to touch his arm, "are you here Ser Brunetto?"
He answered, "Do not be displeased, my Son,
if Brunetto Latini turn and walk a little
downward with you, and lets this herd pass on."
Then I, "I'll go with you, or we can sit
here talking as we used to in the past,
if you desire it, and my guide permit."

"O Son," he answered, "anyone who stands
still a moment will lie here a hundred years,
helpless to brush the sparks off with his hands.
Move on, I'll follow. Soon enough I must
rejoin my little group of friends who walk
with me lamenting their eternal lust."
Then since I dared not leave my bank and move
over the flames of his low path, I bent
my head to walk with reverence and love.
Then he, "What brings you here before your day?
Is it by accident, or Providence?
Who is this man who guides you on your way?"
I answered, "In the world that lies serene
and shining over us, I lost my path,
even before the first young leaves turned green.
Yesterday morning when my steps had come
full circle, this man appeared. He turned me round,
and now he guides me on my journey home."
"O Son," said he, "if you pursue your star,
you cannot fail to reach the glorious harbor.

And if the beautiful world, less sinister,
had let me live a little longer, I too
might have sustained your work and brought you comfort,
seeing how heaven has befriended you.
But that perverted and ungrateful flock
that held the hills with Catiline, and then
descended, hard and sterile as their rock,
to govern Florence, hate you for the good
you do; and rightly! Could they wish to see
the sweet fig ripen on their rotten wood?
Surely, they've earned their reputation: blind,
fratricidal, avaricious, proud.
O root their filthy habits from your mind!
Fortune will load such honors on your back
that Guelph and Ghibelline will hunger for you.
But beat them back from the pasture. Let the pack
run loose, and sicken on the carcasses
that heap the streets, but spare the tender flower,
if one should rise above the swamp and mess—
some flower in which the fragile, sacred seed
of ancient Roman virtue still survives
in Florence, that vulture's nest of lies and greed."
"Master," I said, "you would not walk here now
cut off from human nature, if my prayers
had had an answer. I remember how
I loved you, sitting at your knees—all thought
fixed on your fatherly and gentle face,
when in the world, from hour to hour, you taught
me how a man becomes eternal. O
Master, as long as I draw breath and live,
men shall remember you and what I owe. . . ."

from

Notebook 1967–68

(1969)

Long Summer

1.

At dawn, the crisp goodbye of friends; at night,
enemies reunited, who tread, unmoving,
like circus poodles dancing on a ball—
something inhuman always rising on us,
punching you with embraces, holding out
a hesitant hand, unbending as a broom;
heaping the bright logs brighter, till we sweat
and shine as if anointed with hot oil:
straight alcohol, bright drops, dime-size and silver. . . .
Each day more poignantly resolved to stay,
each day more brutal, oracular and rooted,
dehydrated, and smiling in the fire,
unbandaging his tender, blood-baked foot,
hurt when he kicked aside the last dead bottle.

2.

Humble in victory, chivalrous in defeat,
almost, almost. . . . I bow and watch the ashes
blush, crash, reflect: an age less privileged,
though burdened with its nobles, serfs and Faith.
The possessors. The fires men build live after them,
this night, this night, I elfin, I stonefoot,
walking the wildfire wildrose of those lawns,
filling this cottage window with the same
alluring emptiness, hearing the simmer
of the moon's mildew on the same pile of shells,
fruits of the banquet . . . boiled a brittle lobster-
shell-red, the hollow foreclaw, cracked, sucked dry,
flung on the ash-heap of a soggy carton—
two burnt-out, pinhead, black and popping eyes.

3.

Months of it, and the inarticulate mist so thick
we turned invisible to one another
across the room; the floor, aslant, shot hulling
through thunderheads, gun-cotton dipped in pitch,
salmon, when lighted, as the early moon,
snuffed by the malodorous and frosted murk—
not now! Earth's solid and the sky is light,
yet even on the steadiest day, dead noon,
the sun stockstill like Joshua's in midfield,
I have to brace my hand against a wall
to keep myself from swaying—swaying wall,
straitjacket, hypodermic, helmeted
doctors, one crowd, white-smocked, in panic, hit,
stop, bury the runner on the cleated field.

4.

The vaporish closeness of this two-month fog;
thirty-five summers back, the brightest summer:
the Dealer's Choice, the housebound girls, the fog;
fog lifting. Then, as now, the after curfew
boom of an unknown nightbird, local hemlock
gone black as Roman cypress, the barn-garage
below the tilted Dipper lighthouse-white,
a single misanthropic frog complaining
from the water hazard on the shortest hole;
till morning! Short dreams, short shrift—one second, bright
as burning shavings, scattered bait and ptomaine
caught by the gulls with groans like straining rope;
windjammer pilgrims cowled in rubber hoods,
making for harbor in their yellow bus.

5.

Going the limit on some slip of crabgrass,
vibrating to the everlasting motor,
a hundred yards, two hundred, above the ocean—
or once in New Orleans, when the ceiling fan
wrestled the moisture, and one pajama leg
hung out of reach, caught on a leather blade—
the generation bred to drink the ocean
in that all-possible after Repeal;
all girls then under twenty, and the boys
unearthly with the white blond hair of girls,
crawling the swimming pool's robin's-egg sky;
safe, out of reach. The fall warms vine and wire,
the ant's cool, amber, hyperthyroid eye,
grapes tanning on these tried entanglements.

6.

Shake of the electric fan above our village;
oil truck, refrigerator, or just man,
nightly reloading of the village flesh—
there are worse things than marriage. Men find dates
wherever summer is out, the nights of the swallow
clashing in heat, storm-signal to stay home.
On Court Street, Dyer's Lane, School, Green and Main,
the moon-blanched blacktop fusses like a bosom,
dropping through shade-trees to the shadeless haven—
woman as white as ever. One only knows
her mother, sweatshirt gorged with tennis balls,
still air expiring from the lavish arc—
we too wore armor, strode riveted in cloth,
stiff as the broken clamshell labeled man.

7.
They come, each year more gallant, playing chicken,
then braking to a standstill for a girl;
soft bullets hitting bottles, spars and gulls,
echo and ricochet across the bay—
hardy perennials. Kneedeep in the cowpond,
far from this cockfight, cattle stop and watch us,
then, having had their fill, go back to lapping
soiled water indistinguishable from heaven.
The cattle get through living, but to *live*:
Kokoschka at eighty, saying, "If you last,
you'll see your reputation die three times,
and even three cultures; young girls are always here."
Satyr and chick . . . two fray-winged dragonflies,
clinging to a thistle, too clean to mate.

8.
The shore is pebbled with eroding brick,
seaweed in grizzled furrows—a surf-cast away,
a converted brickyard dormitory; higher,
the blacktop; higher yet, a fish-hawk's nest,
a bungalow, view-hung and staring, with wash
and picture-window—here, like offshoots that
have taken root. Grass shooting overnight,
sticks of dead rotten wood in drifts, the fish
with missing eyes, or heel-print on the belly,
or a gash in the back from a stray hook;
the lawns, the paths, the harbor—stitched with motors,
yawl-engine, outboard, power mower, plowing
the mangle and mash of the monotonous frontier,
bottles of dirt and lighted gasoline.

9.

Two in the afternoon. The restlessness.
Greek Islands. Maine. I have counted the catalogue
of ships down half its length: the blistered canvas,
the metal bowsprits, once pricking up above
the Asian outworks like a wedge of geese,
the migrant yachtsmen, and the fleet in irons. . . .
The iron bell is rocking like a baby,
the high tide's turning on its back exhausted,
the colored, dreaming, silken spinnakers
shove through the patches in the island pine,
as if vegetating millennia of lizards fed
on fern and cropped the treetops . . . or nation of gazelles,
straw-chewers in the African siesta. . . .
I never thought scorn of things; struck fear in no man.

10.

Up north here, in my own country, and free—
look on it with a jaundiced eye, you'll see
the manhood of the sallowing south, *noblesse*
oblige turned redneck, and the fellaheen;
yet sometimes the Nile is wet; life's lived as painted:
those couples, one in love and profit, swaying
their children and their slaves the height of children,
supple and gentle as giraffes or newts;
the waist still willowy, and the paint still fresh;
decorum without hardness; no harness on
the woman, and no armor on the husband,
the red clay Master with his feet of clay,
catwalking lightly through his conquests, leaving
one model, dynasties of faithless copies.

11.

Both my legs hinged on the foreshortened bathtub,
small enough to have been a traveler's . . .
sun baking a bright fluff of balsam needles,
loose yellow swaths; and yet the scene confines;
sun falls on so many, many other things:
someone, Custer, leaping with his wind-gold scalplock,
a furlong or less from the old-style battle,
Sitting Bull's, who sent our hundreds under
in the Indian Summer—Oh that sunlit balsam,
this wizened window, the sea-haze of gauze blue
distance plighting the tree-lip of land to islands—
wives split between a playboy and a drudge.
Who can help us from our nothing to the all,
we aging downstream faster than a scepter can check?

12.

Everyone now is crowing everyone
to put off leaving till the Indian Summer;
and why? Because the others will be gone—
we too, dull drops in the decamping mass,
one in a million buying solitude. . . .
We asked to linger on past fall in Eden;
there must be good in man. Life fears us. Death
keeps our respect by keeping at a distance—
death we've never outdistanced as the Apostle boasted . . .
stream of heady, terrified poured stone,
suburban highway, rural superhighway,
foot of skunkweed, masts of scrub . . . the rich poor. . . .
We are loved by being distant; love-longing
mists the windshield, soothes the eye with milk.

13.

Mischievous fish-shapes without scale or eye
swimming your leaf-green teagown, maternal, autumnal,
swirling six inches past the three-inch heel,
collapsing on us like a parachute,
in a spate of controversial spatter . . . then
exhaustion. We hunger for the ancient fruit,
marriage with its naked artifice;
two practiced animals, close to widower
and widow, greedily bending forward
for the first handgrasp of vermilion leaves,
clinging like bloodclots to the smitten branch—
summer afield and whirling to the tropics,
to the dogdays and dustbowl—men, like ears of corn,
fibrous growths . . . green, sweet, golden, black.

14.

Iced over soon; it's nothing; we're used to sickness;
too little perspiration in the bucket—
in the beginning, polio once a summer. Not that;
each day now the cork more sweetly leaves the bottle,
except a sudden falseness in the breath,
passive participation, dogged sloth,
angrily skirting greener ice, the naught
no longer asset or advantage. Sooner
or later, and the chalk wears out the smile,
this life too long for comfort and too brief
for perfection—Cro-Magnon, dinosaur—
the neverness of meeting nightly like surgeons'
apprentices studying their own skeletons,
old friends and mammoth flesh preserved in ice.

Five Dreams

1. THE OLD ORDER

Eyes shut, I hunt the vision through my eyelids:
first a bull's-head, Cretan black-bronze, high cheekbone
still brave with gilt—too military; I see
a girl's Bacchanalia with a wicker cow's-head;
she died of sleeping pills, but there's a tongue
of silverfoil still sticks in the wicker mouth;
now it's a horse's-head; this is better, it's nervous,
its eyes are string-shot like the bull's; but now,
my bestiary is interrupted: the man,
the beauty in checker trousers, strides the schoolroom;
he is eloquently angry, confiscates the ink-pots;
I wouldn't try this, but perhaps he did right—
a groom tends the black gate to the freestone graveyard—
old law and order that locked at the tap of a glove.

2. AGAMEMNON: A DREAM

As I sleep, their saga comes out clarified:
why for three weeks mother toured the countryside,
buying up earthenware, big pots and urns,
Goliath's potsherds, such as the savage first
archaeologist broke on the first dig—our *own* art:
common the clay, kingly the workmanship.
As I sleep, streams of butane leak from my lighter;
for three weeks mother's foreign in-law kept carving
his chess-sets, leaf green, leaf red, as tall as urns,
modern Viking design for tribal Argos.
The King tripped on his pawns. . . . Suddenly, I see
father's eyes cross and bubble—a whiff of butane,
the muscle of a spitted ox bubbling by the urn. . . .
Can I call the police against my own family?

3. THE HOUSE IN ARGOS

O Christmas tree, how green thy branches—the features
could only be the most conventional,
the hardwood smiles, the Trojan rug's abstraction,
the firelight dancing to the Christmas candles,
the unusual offspring with his usual scowl,
naming all fifty states of Paradise,
with a red, blue, yellow pencil, while his mother,
seasick with marital unhappiness—
she has become the eye of heaven, she hates
her husband swimming like vagueness, like a porpoise,
on the imperial scarlet of the rug. . . .
His corpse in the candles is the fool's-gold lion,
his head is like the rich collection-plate,
singing, "O Christmas tree, how green thy branches . . ."

4. THE NEXT DREAM

"After my marriage, I found myself in constant
companionship with this almost stranger I found
neither agreeable, interesting, nor admirable,
though he was always kind and irresponsible.
The first years after our first child was born,
the daddy was out at sea; that helped, I could bask
in the rest and stimulation of my dreams,
but the courtship was too swift, the disembarkment
dangerously abrupt. I was animal,
healthy, easily tired; I adored luxury,
and should have been an extrovert; I usually
managed to make myself pretty comfortable. . . .
Well," she laughed, "we both were glad to dazzle.
A genius temperament should be handled with care."

5. ONION SKIN

It's the fancy functional things love us best;
not mutely useful, or austerely useless,
they touch our bodies to assume a body.
My half-pound silver ticker had two bopped lids,
a silver lever to be thumbnailed out
at *six*, and *six*, when all hands stopped, and time.
My watch ran to the clockmaker once too often.
Where's Grandfather's gold chain with the snake-head?
They go a-begging; without us, they are gone.
This typing paper pulped in Bucksport, Maine,
onion skin, only merchandised in Maine,
creased when I pulled the last sheet, and seemed to scream,
as if Fortuna bled in the white wood,
first felt the bloody gash that brought my life.

Close the Book

The book is finished and the air is lighter,
I can recognize people in the room;
I touch your pictures, find you in the round.
The cat sits pointing the window from the bedspread,
hooked on the nightlife flashing through the curtain;
he is a *dove* and thinks the lights are pigeons—
flames from the open hearth of Thor and Saul,
arms frescoed on the vaults of the creeping cavern,
missiles no dialectician's hand will turn,
fleshspots for the slung chunks of awk and man.
Children have called the anthropoid, father;
he'd stay home Sunday, and they walked on eggs. . . .
The passage from lower to upper middle age
is quicker than the sigh of a match in the water—
we too were students, and betrayed our hand.

from

Notebook

(1970)

Pastime

1.

Unorthodox sleep in the active hour:
young afternoon, the room, half-darkened, is day,
the raw draft brushing sock and soul.
Like cells of a charging battery, I charge up sleep—
if such sleep lasts, I touch eternity.
This, its pulse-stop, must have been before.
What is true is not real: I here, this bed here, this hour here,
mid-day inscrutable behind these blinds.
When truth says goodmorning, it means goodbye.
Voices drop from forms of distant apartments,
voices of schoolboys . . . they are always ours,
early prep-school; just as this hour is always
optional recess—this has been before:
the sting of touching past time by dropping off.

2.

Labor to pull the raw breath through my closed nostrils
brings back breathing another, rawer air,
drawn freely enough from ice-crust football,
sunlight gilding the golden polo coats
of boys with country seats on the Dutch Hudson.
But why does that light stay? First Form football,
first time being sent on errands by a schoolmate—
Bobby Delano, cousin of Franklin Delano Roosevelt,
escorted drunk off the Presidential yacht,
winner of the football and hockey letters at fifteen;
at fifteen, expelled. He dug my ass with a compass,
and forced me to say my mother was a whore.
My freshman year, he shot himself in Rio,
odius, unknowable, inspired as Ajax.

History

(1973)

History

History has to live with what was here,
clutching and close to fumbling all we had—
it is so dull and gruesome how we die,
unlike writing, life never finishes.
Abel was finished; death is not remote,
a flash-in-the-pan electrifies the skeptic,
his cows crowding like skulls against high-voltage wire,
his baby crying all night like a new machine.
As in our Bibles, white-faced, predatory,
the beautiful, mist-drunken hunter's moon ascends—
a child could give it a face: two holes, two holes,
my eyes, my mouth, between them a skull's no-nose—
O there's a terrifying innocence in my face
drenched with the silver salvage of the mornfrost.

Napoleon

Boston's used bookshops, anachronisms from London,
are gone; it's hard to guess now why I spent
my vacations lugging home his third-hand *Lives*—
shaking the dust from that stationary stock:
cheap deluxe lithographs and gilt-edged pulp
on a man . . . not bloodthirsty, not sparing of blood,
with an eye and *sang-froid* to manage everything;
his iron hand no mere appendage of his mind
for improbable contingencies . . .
for uprooting races, lineages, Jacobins—
the price was paltry . . . three million soldiers dead,
grand opera fixed like morphine in their veins.
Dare we say, he had no moral center?
All gone like the smoke of his own artillery?

Beethoven

Our cookbook is bound like Whitman's *Leaves of Grass*—
gold title on green. I have escaped its death,
take two eggs with butter, drink and smoke;
I live past prudence, not possibility—
who can banquet on the shifting cloud,
lie to friends and tell the truth in print,
be Othello offstage, or Lincoln retired from office?
The vogue of the vague, what can it teach an artist?
Beethoven was a Romantic, but too good;
did kings, republics or Napoleon teach him?
He was his own Napoleon. Did even deafness?
Does the painted soldier in the painting bleed?
Is the captive chorus of *Fidelio* bound?
For a good voice hearing is a torture.

Coleridge

Coleridge stands, he flamed for the one friend. . . .
This shower is warm, I almost breathe-in the rain
horseclopping from fire escape to skylight
down to a dungeon courtyard. In April, New York
has a smell and taste of life. For whom . . . what?
A newer younger generation faces
the firing squad, then their blood is wiped from the pavement. . . .
Coleridge's laudanum and brandy,
his alderman's stroll to positive negation—
his passive courage is paralysis,
standing him upright like tenpins for the strike,
only kept standing by a hundred scared habits . . .
a large soft-textured plant with pith within,
power without strength, an involuntary imposter.

Abraham Lincoln

All day I bang and bang at you in thought,
as if I had the license of your wife. . . .
If War is the continuation of politics—
is politics the discontinuation of murder?
You may have loved underdogs and even mankind,
this one thing made you different from your equals . . .
you, our one genius in politics . . . who followed
the bull to the altar . . . to death in unity.
J'accuse, j'accuse, j'accuse, j'accuse, j'accuse!
Say it in American. Who shot the deserters?
Winter blows sparks in the face of the new God,
who breathes-in fire and dies with cooling faith,
as the firebrand turns black in the black hand,
and the squealing pig darts sidewise from his foot.

Bobby Delano

The labor to breathe that younger, rawer air:
St. Mark's last football game with Groton lost on the ice-crust,
the sunlight gilding the golden polo coats
of boys with country seats on the Upper Hudson.
Why does that stale light stay? First Form hazing,
first day being sent on errands by an oldboy,
Bobby Delano, cousin of Franklin Delano Roosevelt—
deported soused off the Presidential yacht
baritoning *You're the cream in my coffee* . . .
his football, hockey, baseball letter at 15;
at 15, expelled. He dug my ass with a compass,
forced me to say "My mother is a whore."
My freshman year, he shot himself in Rio,
odious, unknowable, inspired as Ajax.

Will Not Come Back
(Volverán)

Dark swallows will doubtless come back killing
the injudicious nightflies with a clack of the beak;
but these that stopped full flight to see your beauty
and my good fortune . . . as if they knew our names—
they'll not come back. The thick lemony honeysuckle,
climbing from the earthroot to your window,
will open more beautiful blossoms to the evening;
but these . . . like dewdrops, trembling, shining, falling,
the tears of day—they'll not come back. . . .
Some other love will sound his fireword for you
and wake your heart, perhaps, from its cool sleep;
but silent, absorbed, and on his knees,
as men adore God at the altar, as I love you—
don't blind yourself, you'll not be loved like that.

Sylvia Plath

A miniature mad talent? Sylvia Plath,
who'll wipe off the spit of your integrity,
rising in the saddle to lash at Auschwitz,
life tearing this or that, *I am a woman?*
Who'll lay the graduate girl in marriage,
queen bee, naked, unqueenly, shaming her shame?
Each English major saying, "*I* am Sylvia,
I hate marriage, I must hate babies."
Even men have a horror of giving birth,
mother-sized babies splitting us in half,
sixty thousand American infants a year,
U.I.D., Unexplained Infant Deaths,
born physically whole and hearty, refuse to live,
Sylvia . . . the expanding torrent of your attack.

Randall Jarrell

The dream went like a rake of sliced bamboo,
slats of dust distracted by a downdraw;
I woke and knew I held a cigarette;
I looked, there was none, could have been none;
I slept off years before I woke again,
palming the floor, shaking the sheets. I saw
nothing was burning. I awoke, I saw
I was holding two lighted cigarettes. . . .
They come this path, old friends, old buffs of death.
Tonight it's Randall, his spark still fire though humble,
his gnawed wrist cradled like *Kitten*. "What kept you so long,
racing the cooling grindstone of your ambition?
You didn't write, you *re*wrote. . . . But tell me,
Cal, why did we live? Why do we die?"

Our Dead Poets

Their lines string out from nowhere, stretch to sorrow.
I think of the others who once had the top billing,
ironclads in our literary havoc,
now even forgotten by malice. "He exists,"
as an old Stalinist luminary said of a friend
sent to Siberia. "Cold helps him to compose."
As a child Jean Stafford stood on a chair to dress;
"It's so much easier." It's easier not to dress,
not brush our teeth, flick off unopened mail.
Sometimes for days I only hear your voices,
the sun of summer will not adorn you again
with her garment of new leaves and flowers . . .
her *nostalgie de la boue* that shelters ape
and protozoa from the rights of man.

T. S. Eliot

Caught between two streams of traffic, in the gloom
of Memorial Hall and Harvard's war-dead. . . . And he:
"Don't you loathe to be compared with your relatives?
I do. I've just found two of mine reviewed by Poe.
He wiped the floor with them . . . and I was *delighted*."
Then on with warden's pace across the Yard,
talking of Pound, "It's balls to say he only
pretends to be Ezra. . . . He's better though. This year,
he no longer wants to rebuild the Temple at Jerusalem.
Yes, he's better. '*You* speak,' he said, when he'd talked two hours.
By then I had absolutely nothing to *say*."
Ah Tom, one muse, one music, had one your luck—
lost in the dark night of the brilliant talkers,
humor and honor from the everlasting dross!

Ezra Pound

Horizontal on a deckchair in the ward
of the criminal mad. . . . A man without shoestrings clawing
the Social Credit broadside from your table, you saying,
". . . here with a black suit and black briefcase; in the brief,
an abomination, Possum's *hommage* to Milton."
Then sprung; Rapallo, and the decade gone;
and three years later, Eliot dead, you saying,
"Who's left alive to understand my jokes?
My old Brother in the arts . . . besides, he was a smash of a poet."
You showed me your blotched, bent hands, saying, "Worms.
When I talked that nonsense about Jews on the Rome
wireless, Olga knew it was shit, and still loved me."
And I, "Who else has been in Purgatory?"
You, "I began with a swelled head and end with swelled feet."

William Carlos Williams

Who loved more? William Carlos Williams,
in collegiate black slacks, gabardine coat,
and loafers polished like rosewood on yachts,
straying stonefoot through his town-end garden,
man and flower seedy with three autumn strokes,
his brown, horned eyes enlarged, an ant's, through glasses;
his Mother, stonedeaf, her face a wizened talon,
her hair the burnt-out ash of lush Puerto Rican grass;
her black, blind, bituminous eye inquisitorial.
"Mama," he says, "which would you rather see here,
me or two blondes?" Then later, "The old bitch
is over a hundred, I'll kick off tomorrow."
He said, "I am sixty-seven, and more
attractive to girls than when I was seventeen."

Robert Frost

Robert Frost at midnight, the audience gone
to vapor, the great act laid on the shelf in mothballs,
his voice is musical and raw—he writes in the flyleaf:
For Robert from Robert, his friend in the art.
"Sometimes I feel too full of myself," I say.
And he, misunderstanding, "When I am low,
I stray away. My son wasn't your kind. The night
we told him Merrill Moore would come to treat him,
he said, 'I'll kill him first.' One of my daughters thought things,
thought every male she met was out to make her;
the way she dressed, she couldn't make a whorehouse."
And I, "Sometimes I'm so happy I can't stand myself."
And he, "When I am too full of joy, I think
how little good my health did anyone near me."

Blizzard in Cambridge

Risen from the blindness of teaching to bright snow,
everything mechanical stopped dead,
taxis no-fares . . . *the wheels grow hot from driving*—
ice-eyelashes, in my spring coat; the subway
too jammed and late to stop for passengers;
snow-trekking the mile from subway end to airport . . .
to all-flights-canceled, fighting queues congealed
to telephones out of order, stamping buses,
rich, stranded New Yorkers staring with the wild, mild eyes
of steers at the foreign subway—then the train home,
jolting with stately grumbling: an hour in Providence,
in New Haven . . . the Bible. In darkness seeing
white arsenic numbers on the tail of a downed plane,
the smokestacks of abandoned fieldguns burning skyward.

For Robert Kennedy 1925–68

Here in my workroom, in its listlessness
of Vacancy, like the old townhouse we shut for summer,
airtight and sheeted from the sun and smog,
far from the hornet yatter of his gang—
is loneliness, a thin smoke thread of vital
air. But what will anyone teach you now?
Doom was woven in your nerves, your shirt,
woven in the great clan; they too were loyal,
and you too were loyal to them, to death.
For them like a prince, you daily left your tower
to walk through dirt in your best cloth. Untouched,
alone in my Plutarchan bubble, I miss
you, you out of Plutarch, made by hand—
forever approaching your maturity.

Dream, the Republican Convention

That night the mustard bush and goldenrod
and more unlikely yellows trod a spiral,
clasped in eviscerating blue china vases
like friendly snakes embracing—cool not cold. . . .
Brotherly, stacked and mean, the great Convention
throws out Americana like dead flowers:
choices, at best, that hurt and cannot cure;
many are chosen, and too few were called. . . .
And yet again, I see the yellow bush rise,
the golds of the goldenrod eclipse their vase
(each summer the young breasts escape the ribcage)
a formation, I suppose, beyond the easel.
What can be is only what will be—
the sun warms the mortician, unpolluted.

After the Democratic Convention

Life, hope, they conquer death, generally, always;
and if the steamroller goes over the flower, the flower dies.
Some are more solid earth; they stood in lines,
blouse and helmet, a creamy de luxe sky-blue—
their music savage and ephemeral.
After five nights of Chicago: police and mob,
I am so tired and had, clichés are wisdom,
the clichés of paranoia. . . . Home in Maine,
the fall of the high tide waves is a straggling, joshing
mell of police . . . they're on the march for me. . . .
How slender and graceful, the double line of trees,
slender, graceful, irregular and underweight,
the young in black folk-fire circles below the trees—
under their shadow, the green grass turns to hay.

The Nihilist as Hero

"All our French poets can turn an inspired line;
who has written six passable in sequence?"
said Valéry. That was a happy day for Satan. . . .
I want words meat-hooked from the living steer,
but a cold flame of tinfoil licks the metal log,
beautiful unchanging fire of childhood
betraying a monotony of vision. . . .
Life by definition breeds on change,
each season we scrap new cars and wars and women.
But sometimes when I am ill or delicate,
the pinched flame of my match turns unchanging green,
a cornstalk in green tails and seeded tassel. . . .
A nihilist wants to live in the world as is,
and yet gaze the everlasting hills to rubble.

For Elizabeth Bishop 4

The new painting must live on iron rations,
rushed brushstrokes, indestructible paint-mix,
fluorescent lofts instead of French *plein air*.
Albert Ryder let his crackled amber moonscapes
ripen in sunlight. His painting was repainting,
his tiniest work weighs heavy in the hand.
Who is killed if the horseman never cry halt?
Have you seen an inchworm crawl on a leaf,
cling to the very end, revolve in air,
feeling for something to reach to something? Do
you still hang your words in air, ten years
unfinished, glued to your notice board, with gaps
or empties for the unimaginable phrase—
unerring Muse who makes the casual perfect?

End of a Year

These conquered kings pass furiously away;
gods die in flesh and spirit and live in print,
each library a misquoted tyrant's home.
A year runs out in the movies, must be written
in bad, straightforward, unscanning sentences—
stamped, trampled, branded on backs of carbons,
lines, words, letters nailed to letters, words, lines—
the typescript looks like a Rosetta Stone. . . .
One more annus mirabilis, its hero *hero demens*,
ill-starred of men and crossed by his fixed stars,
running his ship past sound-spar on the rocks. . . .
The slush-ice on the east bank of the Hudson
is rose-heather in the New Year sunset;
bright sky, bright sky, carbon scarred with ciphers.

from

For Lizzie and Harriet

(1973)

Summer

1.
HARRIET, BORN JANUARY 4, 1957

Half a year, then a year and a half, then
ten and a half—the pathos of a child's fractions, turn-
ing up each summer. Her God a seaslug, God a queen
with forty servants, God—you gave up . . . things whirl
in the chainsaw bite of whatever squares
the universe by name and number. For
the hundredth time, we slice the fog, and round
the village with our headlights on the ground,
like the first philosopher Thales who thought all things water,
and fell in a well . . . trying to find a car
key. . . . It can't be here, and so it must be there
behind the next crook in the road or growth
of fog—there blinded by our feeble beams,
a face, clock-white, still friendly to the earth.

2.
HARRIET

A repeating fly, blueblack, thumbthick—so gross,
it seems apocalyptic in our house—
whams back and forth across the nursery bed
manned by a madhouse of stuffed animals,
not one a fighter. It is like a plane
dusting apple orchards or Arabs on the screen—
one of the mighty . . . one of the helpless. It
bumbles and bumps its brow on this and that,

making a short, unhealthy life the shorter.
I kill it, and another instant's added
to the horrifying mortmain of
ephemera: keys, drift, sea-urchin shells,
you packrat off with joy . . . a dead fly swept
under the carpet, wrinkling to fulfillment.

3.

ELIZABETH

An unaccustomed ripeness in the wood;
move but an inch and moldy splinters fall
in sawdust from the walls' aluminum-paint,
once loud and fresh, now aged to weathered wood.
Squalls of the seagull's exaggerated outcry
dim out in the fog. . . . *Pace, pace.* All day our words
were rusty fish-hooks—wormwood . . . Dear Heart's-Ease,
we rest from all discussion, drinking, smoking,
pills for high blood, three pairs of glasses—soaking
in the sweat of our hard-earned supremacy,
offering a child our leathery love. We're fifty,
and free! Young, tottering on the dizzying brink
of discretion once, you wanted nothing,
but to be old, do nothing, type and think.

4.

THESE WINDS   (HARRIET)

I see these winds, these are the tops of trees,
these are no heavier than green alder bushes;
touched by a light wind, they begin to mingle
and race for instability—too high placed
to stoop to the strife of the brush, these are the winds. . . .

Downstairs, you correct notes at the upright piano,
twice upright this midday Sunday torn from the whole
green cloth of summer; your room was once the laundry,
the loose tap beats time, you hammer the formidable
chords of *The Nocturne*, your second composition.
Since you first began to bawl and crawl
from the unbreakable lawn to this sheltered room, how often
winds have crossed the wind of inspiration—
in these too, the unreliable touch of the all.

5.

HARRIET

Spring moved to summer—the rude cold rain
hurries the ambitious, flowers and youth;
our flash-tones crackle for an hour, and then
we too follow nature, imperceptibly
change our mouse-brown to white lion's mane,
thin white fading to a freckled, knuckled skull,
bronzed by decay, by many, many suns. . . .
Child of ten, three-quarters animal,
three years from Juliet, half Juliet,
already ripened for the night on stage—
beautiful petals, what shall we hope for,
knowing one choice not two is all you're given,
health beyond the measure, dangerous
to yourself, more dangerous to others?

from New York

3.

NEW YEAR'S EVE

By miracle, I left the party half
an hour behind you, reached home five hours drunker,
imagining I would live a million years,
a million quarts drunker than the gods of Jutland—
live through another life and two more wives.
Life is too short to silver over this tarnish.
The gods, employed to haunt and punish husbands,
have no hand for trigger-free distinctions,
their myopia makes all error mortal. . . .
My Darling, prickly hedgehog of the hearth,
chocolates, cherries, hairshirt, pinks and glass—
when we joined in the sublime blindness of courtship,
loving lost all its vice with half its virtue.
Cards will never be dealt to us fairly again.

4.

DEAR SORROW I

If I can't whistle in the dark, why whistle?
One doubts the wisdom of almighty God
casting weak husbands adrift in the hands of a wife.
We need the mighty diaphragm of Job
to jangle grandly. Pain lives in our free discussion,
like the Carlyles fighting meat from the mouth of their dog.
Luckily the Carlyles couldn't bear children—
ours sees me, "Genius, unwise, unbrilliant, weird,"

sees you, "Brilliant, unwise, unweird, nerves."
Barbaric cheek is needed to stay married. . . .
Lizzie, I wake to the hollow of loneliness,
I would cry out *Love, Love,* if I had words:
we are all here for such a short time,
we might as well be good to one another.

8.

HARRIET'S DREAM

"The broom trees twirped by our rosewood bungalow,
not wildlife, these were tropical and straw;
the Gulf fell like a shower on the fiber-sand;
it wasn't the country like our coast of Maine—
on ice for summer. We met a couple, not people,
squared asking Father if he was his name—
none ever said that I was Harriet. . . .
They were laying beach-fires with scarlet sticks and hatchets,
our little bungalow was burning—it
had burned, I was in it. I couldn't laugh,
I was afraid when the ceiling crashed in scarlet;
the shots were boom, the fire was fizz . . . While sleeping
I scrubbed away my scars and blisters, unable
to answer if I had ever hurt."

from Circles

3.

OUR TWENTIETH WEDDING ANNIVERSARY I   (ELIZABETH)

Leaves espaliered jade on our barn's loft window,
sky stretched on a two-pane sash . . . it doesn't open:
stab of roofdrip, this leaf, that leaf twings,
an assault the heartless leaf rejects.
The picture is too perfect for our lives:
in Chardin's stills, the paint bleeds, juice is moving.
We have weathered the wet of twenty years.
Many cripples have won their place in the race;
Immanuel Kant remained unmarried and sane,
no one could Byronize his walk to class.
Often the player outdistances the game. . . .
This week is our first this summer to go unfretted;
we smell as green as the weeds that bruise the flower—
a house eats up the wood that made it.

5.

THE HUMAN CONDITION   (HARRIET)

Should someone human, not just our machinery,
fire on sight, and end the world and us,
surely he'll say he chose the lesser evil—
our wars were simpler than our marriages,
sea monster on sea monster drowning Saturday night—
the acid shellfish that cannot breathe fresh air. . . .
Home things can't stand up to the strain of the earth.
I wake to your cookout and Charles Ives

lulling my terror, lifting my fell of hair,
as David calmed the dark nucleus of Saul.
I'll love you at eleven, twenty, fifty,
young when the century mislays my name—
no date I can name you can be long enough,
the impossible is allied to fact.

6.

THE HARD WAY   (HARRIET)

Don't hate your parents, or your children will hire
unknown men to bury you at your own cost.
Child, forty years younger, will we live to see
your destiny written by our hands rewritten,
your adolescence snap the feathered barb,
the phosphorescence of your wake?
Under the stars, one sleeps, is free from household,
tufts of grass and dust and tufts of grass—
night oriented to the star of youth.
I only learn from error; till lately I trusted
in the practice of my hand. In backward Maine,
ice goes in season to the tropical,
then the mash freezes back to ice, and then
the ice is broken by another wave.

8.

HEAT

For the first time in fifteen years, a furnace
Maine night that would have made summer anywhere,
in Brazil or Boston. The wooden rooms of our house
dry, redoubling their wooden farmhouse smell,
honest wooden ovens shaking with desire.

We feared the pressure was too curative. . . .
Outside, a young seal festers on the beach,
head snapped off, the color of a pig;
much lonelier, this formula for cures.
One nostril shut, my other attenuated—
it's strange tonight I want to pencil myself
do-its on bits of paper. I must remember
to breathe through my mouth. Breathe only from my mouth . . .
as my mouth keeps shutting out the breath of morning.

from Late Summer

3.
BRINGING A TURTLE HOME

On the road to Bangor, we spotted a domed stone,
a painted turtle petrified by fear.
I picked it up. The turtle had come a long walk,
200 millennia understudy to dinosaurs,
then their survivor. A god for the out-of-power. . . .
Faster gods come to Castine, flush yachtsmen who see
hell as a city very much like New York,
these gods give a bad past and worse future to men
who never bother to set a spinnaker;
culture without cash isn't worth their spit.
The laughter on Mount Olympus was always breezy. . . .
Goodnight, little Boy, little Soldier, live,
a toy to your friend, a stone of stumbling to God—
sandpaper Turtle, scratching your pail for water.

4.
RETURNING TURTLE

Weeks hitting the road, one fasting in the bathtub,
raw hamburger mossing in the watery stoppage,
the room drenched with musk like kerosene—
no one shaved, and only the turtle washed.
He was so beautiful when we flipped him over:
greens, reds, yellows, fringe of the faded savage,
the last Sioux, old and worn, saying with weariness,
"Why doesn't the Great White Father put his red

FOR LIZZIE AND HARRIET   177

children on wheels, and move us as he will?"
We drove to the Orland River, and watched the turtle
rush for water like rushing into marriage,
swimming in uncontaminated joy,
lovely the flies that fed that sleazy surface,
a turtle looking back at us, and blinking.

6.

GROWTH   (HARRIET)

"I'm talking the whole idea of life, and boys,
with Mother; and then the heartache, when we're fifty....
You've got to call your *Notebook, Book of the Century,*
but it will take you a century to write,
then I will have to revise it, when you die."
Latin, Spanish, swimming half a mile,
writing a saga with a churl named Eric,
Spanish, Spanish, math and rollerskates;
a love of party dresses, but not boys;
composing something with the bells of *Boris*:
"UNTITLED, would have to be the name of it. . . ."
You grow apace, you grow too fast apace,
too soon adult; no, not adult, like us. . . .
On the telephone, they say, "We're tired, aren't you?"

12.

OUTLIVERS   (HARRIET AND ELIZABETH)

"If we could reverse the world to what it changed
a hundred years ago, or even fifty,
scrupulous drudgery, sailpower, hand-made wars;
God might give us His right to live forever
despite the eroding miracle of science. . . ."

"Was everything that much grander than it is?"
"Nothing seems admirable until it fails;
but it's only people we should miss.
The Goth, retarded epochs like crab and clam,
wept, as we do, for his dead child." We talk
like roommates bleeding night to dawn. You say,
"I hope, of course, you both will outlive me,
but you and Harriet are perhaps like countries
not yet ripe for self-determination."

Obit

Our love will not come back on fortune's wheel—

in the end it gets us, though a man know what he'd have:
old cars, old money, old undebased pre-Lyndon
silver, no copper rubbing through . . . old wives;
I could live such a too long time with mine.
In the end, every hypochondriac is his own prophet.
Before the final coming to rest, comes the rest
of all transcendence in a mode of being, hushing
all becoming. I'm for and with myself in my otherness,
in the eternal return of earth's fairer children,
the lily, the rose, the sun on brick at dusk,
the loved, the lover, and their fear of life,
their unconquered flux, insensate oneness, painful "It was. . . ."
After loving you so much, can I forget
you for eternity, and have no other choice?

from

The Dolphin

(1973)

Fishnet

Any clear thing that blinds us with surprise,
your wandering silences and bright trouvailles,
dolphin let loose to catch the flashing fish . . .
saying too little, then too much.
Poets die adolescents, their beat embalms them,
the archetypal voices sing offkey;
the old actor cannot read his friends,
and nevertheless he reads himself aloud,
genius hums the auditorium dead.
The line must terminate.
Yet my heart rises, I know I've gladdened a lifetime
knotting, undoing a fishnet of tarred rope;
the net will hang on the wall when the fish are eaten,
nailed like illegible bronze on the futureless future.

from Redcliffe Square

2.

WINDOW

Tops of the midnight trees move helter-skelter
to ruin, if passion can hurt the classical
in the limited window of the easel painter—
love escapes our hands. We open the curtains:
a square of white-faced houses swerving, foaming,
the swagger of the world and chalk of London.
At each turn the houses wall the path of meeting,
and yet we meet, stand taking in the storm.
Even in provincial capitals,
storms will rarely enter a human house,
the crude and homeless wet is windowed out.
We stand and hear the pummeling unpurged,
almost uneducated by the world—
the tops of the moving trees move helter-skelter.

4.

OXFORD

We frittered on the long meadow of the Thames,
our shoes laminated with yellow flower—
nothing but the soft of the marsh, the moan of cows,
the rooster-peacock. Before we had arrived,
rising stars illuminated Oxford—
the Aztecs knew these stars would fail to rise
if forbidden the putrification of our flesh,
the victims' viscera laid out like tiles

on fishponds changed to yellow flowers,
the goldfinchnest, the phosphorous of the ocean
blowing ambergris and ambergris,
dolphin kissing dolphin with a smirking smile,
not loving one object and thinking of another.
Our senses want to please us, if we please them.

5.
THE SERPENT

In my dream, my belly is yellow, panels
of mellowing ivory, splendid and still young,
though slightly ragged from defending me.
My tan and green backscales are cool to touch.
For one who has always loved snakes, it is no loss
to change nature. My fall was elsewhere—
how often I made the woman bathe in her waters.
With daylight, I turn small, a small snake
on the river path, arrowing up the jags.
Like this, like this, as the great clock clangs round,
and the green hunter leaps from turn to turn,
a new brass bugle slung on his invisible baldric;
he is groping for trout in the private river,
wherever it opens, wherever it happens to open.

from Hospital 1

I.

SHOES

Too many go express to the house of rest,
buffooning, to-froing on the fringe of being,
one foot in life, and little right to that:
"I had to stop this business going on,
I couldn't attack my doctor anymore,
he lost his nerve for running out on life. . . ."
"Where I am not," we chime, "is where I am."
Dejection washes our pollution bare.
My shoes? Did they walk out on me last night,
and streak into the glitter of the blear?
I see two dirty white, punctured tennis-shoes,
empty and planted on the one-man path.
I have no doubt where they will go. They walk
the one life offered from the many chosen.

Records

"... I was playing records on Sunday,
arranging all my records, and I came
on some of your voice, and started to suggest
that Harriet listen: then immediately
we both shook our heads. It was like hearing
the voice of the beloved who had died.
All this is a new feeling ... I got the letter
this morning, the letter you wrote me Saturday.
I thought my heart would break a thousand times,
but I would rather have read it a thousand times
than the detached unreal ones you wrote before—
you doomed to know what I have known with you,
lying with someone fighting unreality—
love vanquished by his mysterious carelessness."

Mermaid

1.

I have learned what I wanted from the mermaid
and her singeing conjunction of tail and grace.
Deficiency served her. What else could she do?
Failure keeps snapping up transcendence,
bubble and bullfrog boating on the surface,
belly lustily lagging three inches lowered—
the insatiable fiction of desire.
None swims with her and breathes the air.
A mermaid flattens soles and picks a trout,
knife and fork in chainsong at the spine,
weeps white rum undetectable from tears.
She kills more bottles than the ocean sinks,
and serves her winded lovers' bones in brine,
nibbled at recess in the marathon.

2.

Baudelaire feared women, and wrote, "Last night, I slept
with a hideous negress." Woe to Black Power,
woe to French women and the Academicians.
Why do I blush the moon with what I say?
Alice-in-Wonderland straight gold hair,
fair-featured, curve and bone from crown to socks,
bulge eyes bigger than your man's closed fist,
slick with humiliation when dismissed—
you are packaged to the grave with me,
where nothing's opened by the addressee . . .
almost a year and almost my third wife,
by accepting, by inviting, by surmounting,
rushing the music when the juice goes dead—
float like a butterfly and sting like a bee.

3.
Our meetings are no longer like a screening;
I see the nose on my face is just a nose,
your *bel occhi grandi* are just eyes
in the photo of you arranged as figurehead
or mermaid on the prow of a Roman dory,
bright as the morning star or a blond starlet.
Our twin black and tin Ronson butane lighters
knock on the sheet, are what they are,
too many, and burned too many cigarettes. . . .
Night darkens without your necessary call,
it's time to turn your pictures to the wall;
your moon-eyes water and your nervous throat
gruffs my directive, "*You must go now go.*"
Contralto mermaid, and stone-deaf at will.

4.
I see you as a baby killer whale,
free to walk the seven seas for game,
warmhearted with an undercoat of ice,
a nerve-wrung back . . . all muscle, youth, intention,
and skill expended on a lunge or puncture—
hoisted now from conquests and salt sea
to flipper-flapper in a public tank,
big deal for Sunday children. . . . My blind love—
on the Via Veneto, a girl
counting windows in a glass café,
now frowning at her menu, now counting out
neanderthals flashed like shorebait on the walk. . . .
Your stamina as *inside-right* at school
spilled the topheavy boys, and keeps you pure.

5.
One wondered who would see and date you next,
and grapple for the danger of your hand.
Will money drown you? Poverty, though now
in fashion, debases women as much as wealth.
You use no scent, dab brow and lash with shoeblack,
willing to face the world without more face.
I've searched the rough black ocean for you,
and saw the turbulence drop dead for you,
always lovely, even for those who had you,
Rough Slitherer in your grotto of haphazard.
I lack manhood to finish the fishing trip.
Glad to escape beguilement and the storm,
I thank the ocean that hides the fearful mermaid—
like God, I almost doubt if you exist.

from Exorcism

2.

This morning, as if I were home in Boston, snow,
the pure witchery-bitchery of kindergarten winters;
my window whitens like a movie screen,
glaring, specked, excluding rival outlook—
I can throw what I want on this blank screen,
but only the show already chosen shows:
Melodrama with her stiletto heel
dancing bullet wounds in the parquet.
My words are English, but the plot is hexed:
one man, two women, the common novel plot . . .
what you love you are. . . .
You can't carry your talent with you like a suitcase.
Don't you dare mail us the love your life denies;
do you really know *what you have done?*

Plotted

Planes arc like arrows through the highest sky,
ducks *V* the ducklings across a puckered pond;
Providence turns animals to things.
I roam from bookstore to bookstore browsing books,
I too maneuvered on a guiding string
as I execute my written plot.
I feel how Hamlet, stuck with the Revenge Play
his father wrote him, went scatological
under this clotted London sky.
Catlike on a paper parapet,
he declaimed the words his prompter fed him,
knowing convention called him forth to murder,
loss of free will and license of the stage.
Death's not an event in life, it's not lived through.

The Couple

"Twice in the past two weeks I think I met
Lizzie in the recurrent dream.
We were out walking. *What sort of street*, you ask,
fair or London? It was our own street.
What did you hear and say? We heard ourselves.
The sidewalk was two feet wide. We, arm in arm,
walked, squelching the five-point oakleaves under heel—
happily, they melted under heel.
Our manner had some intimacy in my dream.
What were you doing on this honeymoon?
Our conversation had a simple plot,
a story of a woman and a man
versifying her tragedy—
we were talking like sisters . . . you did not exist."

Mermaid Emerging

The institutions of society
seldom look at a particular—
Degas's snubnosed dancer swings on high,
legging the toplights, never leaving stage,
enchanting lovers of art, discerning none.
Law fit for all fits no one like a glove. . . .
Mermaid, why are you another species?
"Because, you, I, everyone is unique."
Does anyone ever make you do anything?
"Do this, do that, do nothing; you're not chained.
I am a woman or I am a dolphin,
the only animal man really loves,
I spout the smarting waters of joy in your face—
rough-weather fish, who cuts your nets and chains."

from Another Summer

I.
WILDROSE

A mongrel image for all summer, our scene at breakfast:
a bent iron fence of straggly wildrose glowing
below the sausage-rolls of new-mown hay—
Sheridan splashing in his blue balloon tire:
whatever he touches he's told not to touch
and whatever he reaches tips over on him.
Things have gone on and changed, the next oldest
daughter bleaching her hair three shades lighter with beer—
but if you're not a blonde, it doesn't work. . . .
Sleeping, the always finding you there with day,
the endless days revising our revisions—
everyone's wildrose? . . . And our golden summer
as much as such people can. When most happiest
how do I know I can keep any of us alive?

On the End of the Phone

My sidestepping and obliquities, unable
to take the obvious truth on any subject—
why do I do what I do not want to say,
able to understand and not to hear?
Your rapier voice—I have had so much—
hundred words a minute, piercing and thrilling . . .
the invincible lifedrive of everything alive,
ringing down silver dollars with each word. . . .
Love wasn't what went wrong, we kept our daughter;
what a good father is is no man's boast—
to be still friends when we're no longer children. . . .
Why am I talking from the top of my mouth?
I am talking to you transatlantic,
we're almost talking in one another's arms.

Dolphin

My Dolphin, you only guide me by surprise,
captive as Racine, the man of craft,
drawn through his maze of iron composition
by the incomparable wandering voice of Phèdre.
When I was troubled in mind, you made for my body
caught in its hangman's-knot of sinking lines,
the glassy bowing and scraping of my will. . . .
I have sat and listened to too many
words of the collaborating muse,
and plotted perhaps too freely with my life,
not avoiding injury to others,
not avoiding injury to myself—
to ask compassion . . . this book, half fiction,
an eelnet made by man for the eel fighting—

my eyes have seen what my hand did.

from

Day by Day

(1977)

Last Walk?

That unhoped-for Irish sunspoiled April day
heralded the day before
by corkscrews of the eternal
whirling snow that melts and dies
and leaves the painted green pasture marsh—
and the same green . . . We could even imagine
we enjoined our life's great change then—
hand in hand with balmy smiles
graciously belittling our headlong reverse.

We walked to an artificial pond
dammed at both ends to reflect the Castle—
a natural composition for the faded colorist
on calm bright days or brighter nights.
At first we mistook the pond for a lull in the river—
the Liffey, torrential, wild,
accelerated to murder,
wider here than twenty miles downhill to Dublin—
black, rock-kneed, crashing on crags—
by excessive courage married to the ocean.

"Those swans," you said, "if one loses its mate,
the other dies. This spring a Persian exile
killed one cruelly, and its mate
refused to be fed—
It roused an explosion of xenophobia
when it died."
Explosion is growing common here;
Yet everything about the royal swan
is silly, overstated, a luxury toy
beyond the fortunate child's allowance.

We sat and watched a mother swan
Enthroned like a colossal head of Pharaoh
on her messy double goose-egg nest of sticks.
The male swan had escaped
their safe, stagnant, matriarchal pond
and gallanted down the stout-enriched rapids to Dublin,
smirking drunkenly, racing bumping,
as if to show a king had a right to be too happy.

I meant to write about our last walk.
We had nothing to do but gaze—
seven years, now nothing but a diverting smile,
dalliance by a river, a speeding swan . . .
the misleading promise
to last with joy as long as our bodies,
nostalgia pulverized by thought,
nomadic as yesterday's whirling snow,
all whiteness splotched.

Square of Black

On this book, large enough to write on,
is a sad, black, actual photograph
of Abraham Lincoln and Tad in 1861,
father and son,
their almost matching silver watchchains,
as they stare into the blank ledger,
its murders and failures . . . they.
Old Abe, and old at 52—
in life, in office, no lurking illusion,
clad for the moment in robes of splendor,
passed him unchallenged . . .
Only in a dream was he able to hear
his voice in the East Room of the White House
saying over his own dead body:
"Lincoln is dead."

Dreams, they've had their vogue,
so alike in their modernist invention,
so dangerously distracted by commonplace,
their literal insistence on the letter,
trivia indistinguishable from tragedy—
his monstrous melodrama terminating
at a playhouse . . . dreaming, overhearing
his own voice,
the colloquial sibilance of the circuit-court,
once freedom, the law and home to Lincoln—
shot while sleeping through the final act.

Fortunately
I only dream inconsequence.

Last night I saw a little
flapping square of pure black cloth.
It flew to the corners of my bedroom,
hugging, fluttering there coquettishly—
a bat, if wing and pelt could be one-color black.
It was a mouse. (So my dream explained.)
It taught me to feed and tame it
with nagging love . . . only existing
in my short dream's immeasurable leisure.

The Day

It's amazing
the day is still here
like lightning on an open field,
terra firma and transient
swimming in variation,
fresh as when man first broke
like the crocus all over the earth.

From a train, we saw cows
strung out on a hill
at differing heights,
one sex, one herd,
replicas in hierarchy—
the sun had turned
them noonday bright.

They were child's daubs in a book
I read before I could read.

They fly by like a train window:
flash-in-the-pan moments
of the Great Day,
the *dies illa*,
when we lived momently
together forever
in love with our nature—

as if in the end,
in the marriage with nothingness,
we could ever escape
being absolutely safe.

Marriage

I.
We were middle-class and verismo
enough to suit Van Eyck,
when we crowded together in Maidstone,
patriarch and young wife
with our three small girls
to pose in Sunday-best.
The shapeless comfort of your flowered frock
was transparent against the light,
but the formal family photograph in color
shows only a rousing brawn of shoulder
to tell us you were pregnant.

Even there, Sheridan, though unborn,
was a center of symmetry;
even then he was growing in hiding
toward gaucheness and muscle—
to be a war-
chronicler of vast inaccurate memory.
Later, his weird humor
made him elf and dustman,
like him, early risers.
This summer, he is a soldier—
unlike father or mother,
or anyone he knows,
he can choose both sides:
Redcoat, Minuteman, or George the Third . . .
the ambivalence of the Revolution that made him
half-British, half-American.

II.
I turn to the *Arnolfini Marriage*,
and see
Van Eyck's young Italian merchant
was neither soldier nor priest.
In an age of Faith,
he is not abashed to stand weaponless,
long-faced and dwindling
in his bridal bedroom.
Half-Jewish, perhaps,
he is freshly married,
and exiled for his profit to Bruges.
His wife's with child;
he lifts a hand,
thin and white as his face
held up like a candle to bless her . . .
smiling, swelling, blossoming . . .

Giovanni and Giovanna—
even in an age of costumes,
they seem to flash their fineness . . .
better dressed than kings.

The picture is too much like their life—
a crisscross, too many petty facts,
this bedroom
with one candle still burning in the candelabrum,
and peaches blushing on the windowsill,
Giovanni's high-heeled raw wooden slippers
thrown on the floor by her smaller ones . . .
dyed *sang de boeuf*
to match the restless marital canopy.

They are rivals in homeliness and love;
her hand lies like china in his,

her other hand
is in touch with the head of her unborn child.
They wait and pray,
as if the airs of heaven
that blew on them when they married
were now a common visitation,
not a miracle of lighting
for the photographer's sacramental instant.

Giovanni and Giovanna,
who will outlive him by 20 years . . .

Logan Airport, Boston

Your blouse,
Concord grapes on white,
a souvenir you snatched up at the airport,
shone blindingly up the gangway
to a sky overcrowded at rush-hour.
Below the flying traffic,
thin, dwindling yellow trees were feverish,
as if frightened
by your limitless prospect on the blue.

I see you, you are hardly there—
it's as though I watched a painter
do sketches of your head
that by some consuming fire
erased themselves,
until I stared at a blank sheet.

Now in the brown air of our rental,
I need electricity even on fair days,
as I decamp from window to window
to catch the sun.
I am blind with seeing;
the toys you brought home like groceries
firetrap on the stairs.

Is it cynical to deliquesce,
as Adam did in age,
though outwardly goldleaf,
true metal, and make-up?

Our mannerisms harden—
a bruise is immortal,
the instant egg on my shin
I got from braking a car
too sharply a year ago
stays firm brown and yellow,
the all-weather color for death.

I cannot bring back youth with a snap of my belt,
I cannot touch you—
your absence is presence,
the undrinkable blaze
of the sun on both shores of the airport.

Bright sun of my bright day,
I thank God for being alive—
a way of writing I once thought heartless.

Grass Fires

In the realistic memory
the memorable must be forgone;
it never matters,
except in front of our eyes.

I made it a warning,
a cure, that stabilized nothing.
We cannot recast the faulty drama,
play the child,
unable to align
his toppling, elephantine script,
the hieroglyphic letters
he sent home.

I hold big kitchen matches to flaps of frozen grass
to smoke a rabbit from its hole—
then the wind bites them, then they catch,
the grass catches, fire everywhere,
everywhere
inextinguishable roots,
the tree grandfather planted for his shade,
combusting, towering
over the house he anachronized with stone.

I can't tell you how much larger
and more important it was than I,
how many summers before conscience
I enjoyed it.

My grandfather towered above me,
"You damned little fool,"
nothing to quote, but for him original.
The fire-engines deployed with stage bravado,
yet it was I put out the fire,
who slapped it to death with my scarred leather jacket.
I snuffed out the inextinguishable root,
I—
really I can do little,
as little now as then,
about the infernal fires—
I cannot blow out a match.

Suburban Surf

(After Caroline's Return)

You lie in my insomniac arms,
as if you drank sleep like coffee.

Then,
like a bear tipping a hive for honey,
you shake the pillow for French cigarettes.

No conversation—
then suddenly as always cars
helter-skelter for feed like cows—

suburban surf come alive,

diamond-faceted like your eyes,
glassy, staring lights
lighting the way they cannot see—

friction, constriction etc.
the racket killing
gas like alcohol.

Long, unequal whooshing waves
break in volume,
always very loud enough to hear

méchants, mechanical—

soothe, delay, divert
the crescendo always surprisingly attained
in a panic of breathlessness—

too much assertion and skipping
of the heart to greet the day . . .
the truce with uncertain heaven.
A false calm is the best calm.

In noonday light,
the cars are tin, stereotype and bright,
a farce
of their former selves at night—
invisible as exhaust,
personal as animals.

Gone
the sweet agitation of the breath of Pan.

Shaving

Shaving's the one time I see my face,
I see it aslant as a carpenter's problem—
though I have gaunted a little,
always the same face
follows my hand with thirsty eyes.

Never enough hours in a day—
I lie confined and groping,
monomaniacal,
jealous even a shadow's intrusion—
a nettle
impossible to deflect . . .
unable to follow the drift
of children, their blurting third-degree.

For me,
a stone is as inflammable as a paper match.

The household comes to a stop—
you too, head bent,
inking, crossing out . . . frowning
at times with a face open as a sunflower.

We are lucky to have done things as one.

Caroline in Sickness

Tonight the full moon is stopped by trees
or the wallpaper between our windows—
on the threshold of pain,
light doesn't exist,
and yet the glow is smarting
enough to read a Bible
to keep awake and awake.
You are very sick,
you remember how the children,
you and your cousin,
Miss Fireworks and Miss Icicle,
first drove alone with learners' cards
in Connemara, and popped a paper bag—
the rock that broke your spine.
Thirty years later you still suffer
your spine's spasmodic, undercover life . . .
Putting off a luncheon,
you say into the telephone,
"Next month, if I'm still walking."
I move to keep moving;
the cold white wine is dis-spirited—
Moon, stop from dark apprehension . . .
shine as is your custom,
scattering this roughage to find sky.

Seesaw

The night dark before its hour—
heavily, steadily,
the rain lashes and sprinkles
to complete its task—
as if assisting
the encroachments of our bodies
we occupy but cannot cure.

Sufferer, how can you help me,
if I use your sickness
to increase my own?

Will we always be
one up, the other down,
one hitting bottom, the other
flying through the trees—
seesaw inseparables?

Ten Minutes

The single sheet keeps shifting on the double bed,
the more I kick it smooth, the less it covers;
it is the bed I made.
Others have destinations, my train is aimless.
I know I will fall off into the siding and thistle—
imagining the truth will hide my lies.

Mother under one of her five-minute spells
had a flair for total recall,
and told me, item by item, person by person,
how my relentless, unpredictable selfishness
had disappointed and removed
anyone who tried to help—
but I cannot correct the delicate compass-needle
so easily set ajar.

I am companionless;
occasionally, I see a late, suicidal headlight
burn on the highway and vanish.
Now the haunted vacancy fills with friends—
they are waspishly familiar and aggrieved,
a rattling makeshift of mislaid faces,
a whiplash of voices. They cry,
"Can you love me, can you love me?
Oh hidden in your bubble and protected by your wife,
and luxuriously nourished without hands,
you wished us dead,
but vampires are too irreplaceable to die."

They stop, as cars that have the greenlight
stop, and let a pedestrian go . . .
Though I work nightshift,
there's no truth in this processing of words—
the dull, instinctive glow inside me
refuels itself, and only blackens
such bits of paper brought to feed it . . .

My frightened arms
anxiously hang out before me like bent L's,
as if I feared I was a laughingstock,
and wished to catch and ward you off . . .
This is becoming a formula:
after the long, dark passage,
I offer you my huddle of flesh and dismay.
"This time it was all night," I say.
You answer, "Poseur,
why, you haven't been awake ten minutes."

●　　●　　●

I grow too merry,
when I stand in my nakedness to dress.

Notice

The resident doctor said,
"We are not deep in ideas, imagination or enthusiasm—
how can we help you?"
I asked,
"These days of only poems and depression—
what can I do with them?
Will they help me to notice
what I cannot bear to look at?"

The doctor is forgotten now
like a friend's wife's maiden-name.
I am free
to ride elbow to elbow on the rush-hour train
and copy on the back of a letter,
as if alone:
"When the trees close branches and redden,
their winter skeletons are hard to find—"
to know after long rest
and twenty miles of outlying city
that the much-heralded spring is here,
and say,
"Is this what you would call a blossom?"
Then home—I can walk it blindfold.
But we must notice—
we are designed for the moment.

Shifting Colors

I fish until the clouds turn blue,
weary of self-torture, ready to paint
lilacs or confuse a thousand leaves,
as landscapists must.

My eye returns to my double,
an ageless big white horse,
slightly discolored by dirt
cropping the green shelf diagonal
to the artificial troutpond—
unmoving, it shifts as I move,
and works the whole field in the course of the day.

Poor measured, neurotic man—
animals are more instinctive virtuosi.

Ducks splash deceptively like fish;
fish break water with the wings of a bird to escape.

A hissing goose sways in stationary anger;
purple bluebells rise in ledges on the lake.

A single cuckoo gifted with a pregnant word
shifts like the sun from wood to wood.

All day my miscast troutfly buzzes about my ears
and empty mind.

But nature is sundrunk with sex—
how could a man fail to notice, man

the one pornographer among the animals?
I seek leave unimpassioned by my body,
I am too weak to strain to remember, or give
recollection the eye of a microscope. I see
horse and meadow, duck and pond,
universal consolatory
description without significance,
transcribed verbatim by my eye.

This is not the directness that catches
everything on the run and then expires—
I would write only in response to the gods,
like Mallarmé who had the good fortune
to find a style that made writing impossible.

Unwanted

Too late, all shops closed—
I alone here tonight on *Antabuse*,
surrounded only by iced white wine and beer,
like a sailor dying of thirst on the Atlantic—
one sip of alcohol might be death,
death for joy.
Yet in this tempting leisure,
good thoughts drive out bad;
causes for my misadventure, considered
for forty years too obvious to name,
come jumbling out
to give my simple autobiography a plot.

I read an article on a friend,
as if recognizing my obituary:
"Though his mother loved her son consumingly,
she lacked a really affectionate nature;
so he always loved what he missed."
This was John Berryman's mother, not mine.

Alas, I can only tell my own story—
talking to myself, or reading, or writing,
or fearlessly holding back nothing from a friend,
who believes me for a moment
to keep up conversation.

I was surer, wasn't I, once . . .
and had flashes when I first found
a humor for myself in images,
farfetched misalliance
that made evasion a revelation?

Dr. Merrill Moore, the family psychiatrist,
had unpresentable red smudge eyebrows,
and no infirmity for tact—
in his conversation or letters,
each phrase a new
paragraph,
implausible as the million
sonnets he rhymed into his dictaphone,
or dashed on windshield writing-pads,
while waiting out a stoplight—
scattered pearls, some true.
Dead he is still a mystery,
once a crutch to writers in crisis.
I am two-tongued, I will not admit
his Tennessee rattling saved my life.
Did he become mother's lover
and prey
by rescuing her from me?
He was thirteen years her junior . . .
When I was in college, he said, "You know
you were an unwanted child?"
Was he striking my parents to help me?
I shook him off the scent by pretending
anyone is unwanted in a medical sense—
lust our only father . . . and yet
in that world where an only child
was a scandal—
unwanted before I am?

That year Carl Jung said to mother in Zurich,
"If your son is as you have described him,
he is an incurable schizophrenic."

In 1916
father on sea-duty, mother with child

in one house with her affectionate mother-in-law,
unconsuming, already consumptive . . .
bromidic to mother . . . Mother,
I must not blame you for carrying me in you
on your brisk winter lunges across
the desperate, refusey Staten Island beaches,
their good view skyscrapers on Wall Street . . .
for yearning seaward, far from any home, and saying,
"I wish I were dead, I wish I were dead."
Unforgivable for a mother to tell her child—
but you wanted me to share your good fortune,
perhaps, by recapturing the disgust of those walks;
your credulity assumed we survived,
while weaklings fell with the dead and dying.

That consuming love,
woman's everlasting *cri de coeur*,
"When you have a child of your own, you'll know."
Her dowry for her children . . .

One thing is certain—compared with my wives,
mother was stupid. Was she?
Some would not have judged so—
among them, her alcoholic patients,
those raconteurish, old Boston young men,
whose fees, late in her life
and to everyone's concern,
she openly halved with Merrill Moore.
Since time out of mind, mother's gay hurting
assessments of enemies and intimates
had made her a formidable character
to her "reading club," seven ladies,
who since her early twenties
met once a week through winters
in their sitting rooms for confidence and tea—

she couldn't read a book . . .
How many of her statements began with,
But Papá always said or *Oh Bobby* . . .
if she Byronized her father and son,
she saw her husband as a valet sees through a master.

She was stupider than my wife . . .
When I was three months,
I rocked back and forth howling
for weeks, for weeks each hour . . .
Then I found the thing I loved most
was the anorexia Christ
swinging on Nellie's gaudy rosary.
It disappeared, I said nothing,
but mother saw me poking strips of paper
down a floor-grate to the central heating.
"Oh Bobby, do you want to set us on fire?"
"Yes . . . that's where Jesus is." I smiled.

Is the one unpardonable sin
our fear of not being wanted?
For this, will mother go on cleaning house
for eternity, and making it unlivable?
Is getting well ever an art,
or art a way to get well?

Thanks-Offering for Recovery

The airy, going house grows small
tonight, and soft enough to be crumpled up
like a handkerchief in my hand.
Here with you by this hotbed of coals,
I am the *homme sensuel*, free
to turn my back on the lamp, and work.
Something has been taken off,
a wooden winter shadow—
goodbye nothing. I give thanks, thanks—
thanks too for this small
Brazilian *ex voto*, this primitive head
sent me across the Atlantic by my friend . . .
a corkweight thing,
to be offered *Deo gratias* in church
on recovering from head-injury or migraine—
now mercifully delivered in my hands,
though shelved awhile unnoticing and unnoticed.
Free of the unshakable terror that made me write . . .
I pick it up, a head holy and unholy,
tonsured or damaged,
with gross black charcoaled brows and stern eyes
frowning as if they had seen the splendor
times past counting . . . unspoiled,
solemn as a child is serious—
light balsa wood the color of my skin.
It is all childcraft, especially
its shallow, chiseled ears,
crudely healed scars lumped out
to listen to itself, perhaps, not knowing
it was made to be given up.

Goodbye nothing. Blockhead,
I would take you to church,
if any church would take you . . .
This winter, I thought
I was created to be given away.

Epilogue

Those blessed structures, plot and rhyme—
why are they no help to me now
I want to make
something imagined, not recalled?
I hear the noise of my own voice:
The painter's vision is not a lens,
it trembles to caress the light.
But sometimes everything I write
with the threadbare art of my eye
seems a snapshot,
lurid, rapid, garish, grouped,
heightened from life,
yet paralyzed by fact.
All's misalliance.
Yet why not say what happened?
Pray for the grace of accuracy
Vermeer gave to the sun's illumination
stealing like the tide across a map
to his girl solid with yearning.
We are poor passing facts,
warned by that to give
each figure in the photograph
his living name.

from

Last Poems

(1977)

Summer Tides

gradually veering, the Lake are when I hand
Then others, misnatures, such
tumbles on a long lead of

Tonight
I watch the incoming moon swim
under three agate veins of cloud,
casting crisps of false silver-plate
to the thirsty granite fringe of the shore.
Yesterday, the sun's gregarious sparklings;
tonight, the moon has no satellite.
All this spendthrift, in-the-house summer,
our yacht-jammed harbor
lay unattempted—
pictorial to me like your portrait.
I wonder who posed you so artfully
for it in the prow of his Italian skiff,
like a maiden figurehead without legs to fly.
Time lent its wings. Last year
our drunken quarrels had no explanation,
except everything, except everything.
Did the oak provoke the lightning,
when we heard its boughs and foliage fall? . . .
My wooden beach-ladder swings by one bolt,
and repeats its single creaking rhythm—
I cannot go down to the sea.
After so much logical interrogation,
I can do nothing that matters.
The east wind carries disturbance for leagues—
I think of my son and daughter,
and three stepdaughters
on far-out ledges
washed by the dreaded clock-clock of the waves . . .

gradually rotting the bulwark where I stand.
Their father's unmotherly touch
trembles on a loosened rail.

Index of Titles
and First Lines

Poem titles are *italicized*.

A brackish reach of shoal off Madaket,—, 4
A miniature mad talent? Sylvia Plath, 152
A mongrel image for all summer, our scene at breakfast, 195
Abraham Lincoln, 149
After the Democratic Convention, 162
Again and then again . . . the year is born, 3
All day I bang and bang at you in thought, 149
"All our French poets can turn an inspired line, 163
Another Summer, 195
Any clear thing that blinds us with surprise, 183
At Beverly Farms, a portly, uncomfortable boulder, 68
At dawn, the crisp goodbye of friends; at night, 127

Back and forth, back and forth, 97
Beethoven, 147
Between the Porch and the Altar, 10
Beyond the Alps, 25
Blizzard in Cambridge, 159
Bobby Delano, 150
Boston's used bookshops, anachronisms from London, 146
BRINGING A TURTLE HOME, 177
Brunetto Latini, 123
Burnished, burned-out, still burning as the year, 103
Buttercups, 9
By miracle, I left the party half, 172

Caligula, 108
Caroline in Sickness, 216